CONTRACT AND RISK MANAGEMENT

FOR

SUPPLY CHAIN MANAGEMENT

PROFESSIONALS

X. Paul Humbert, Esq.
Robert C. Mastice, MSME

FIRST EDITION

THE HUMBERT GROUP, LLC

Note:

The information provided in this book covers concepts and principles that have stood the test of time. However, all transactions are fact specific and case sensitive. In addition, this text is not intended to provide legal advice or guidance regarding specific transactions. Consult your subject matter experts who can assist you in their respective areas of expertise and experience regarding the law, insurance, risk management, tax and accounting issues for specific commercial transactions.

Printed in the United States of America

Copyright © 2014 X. Paul Humbert, Esq.
All rights reserved.
ISBN: 0615956718
ISBN 13: 9780615956718

Library of Congress Control Number: 2014901576

X. Paul Humbert
Summit, NJ

TABLE OF CONTENTS

TABLE OF CONTENTS

PREFACE

What Will This Book Do for You? This book provides a survival manual for anyone involved in the crafting, structuring, negotiating, supporting or managing contracts involving commercial transactions of goods, services or both. It blends the practical with general legal principles and highlights best practices for supply chain professionals and anyone else involved, directly or indirectly, with the generation or management of contracts from cradle-to-grave. Even commercially wise and sophisticated organizations can be untrained and unaware of certain gaps and traps in the management of their contracts.

This book addresses those pitfalls and provides lessons learned and guidance that are not typically taught at the college or even graduate school level. Experience can be hard and expensive to come by and this book provides a concentrated dose of experience that immediately raises the reader's level of sophistication and awareness for gaps and traps while providing practical solutions to pitfalls that can haunt any organization. Left unchecked, these pitfalls can lead to dysfunction and confusion; both of which can be an expensive proposition in today's competitive and uncertain economic environment.

Who Should Use this Book? Supply Chain Management Professionals, Risk Managers, Insurance Experts, Project Managers, Purchasing Agents,

Contract Administrators, Executives and any business or technical professionals who are involved with developing, managing or implementing projects, purchases or any complex transaction or procurement where cost, schedule and scope certainty are important.

What Does This Book Cover? This book covers how the relationship of the parties affects commercial transactions and addresses the importance of upholding the integrity of the process and the contract by understanding key supply chain best practices. The book focuses on contracting strategies and approaches including how to structure requests for proposals and instructions to bidders as well as key considerations in pricing and pricing adjustments, risk management tools and techniques, the importance of defining the deliverables and outcomes, negotiation strategies and techniques, negotiating warranties and remedies, applying leadership and influencing skills to the process, how to implement sound change management as well as capturing and applying past lessons learned. In addition, special attention is given to the importance of sound "kick off" and "close out", including termination for cause or convenience techniques and other best practices.

ABOUT THE AUTHORS

X. Paul Humbert. Esq.

Paul Humbert is President of the Humbert Group, LLC, which provides consulting services to global procurement clients with particular emphasis on: complex negotiations, strategic alliances, process improvement, risk management techniques, project management assistance, training and coaching, as well as post-execution contract management including dispute resolution. Paul holds degrees in both business and law and has extensive experience in these areas. He is an expert in structuring agreements and contract management procedures that are clear and minimize the risk of claims or non-conforming deliverables.

In addition to assisting clients, Paul also teaches at the graduate school level. He is a part time lecturer at the Rutgers University Graduate School of Business and has also served as Adjunct Professor at both Seton Law School and Monmouth College where he taught legal and business courses. Paul has also served as an arbiter for the American Arbitration Association. Paul is a frequent lecturer and guest speaker.

Contact Information: xphumbert@thehumbertgroup.net

Robert C. Mastice, MSME

Robert C. Mastice is Principal / Managing Director of Tri-Power Consulting Services, LLC ("Tri-Power"). Tri-Power serves fortune 500 companies in three areas: (a) project based contracting management / document management, (b) contingent labor contracting labor services for managed service programs (MSPs) and (c) business process modeling using custom built IT applications. Tri-Power's affiliate, Tri-Power Design, LLC provides electromechanical design, engineering, prototyping and manufacturing service to global companies for medical devices, consumer products as well as custom one-of-a-kind machine design, engineering and fabrication.

Robert has years of experience in contract creation, negotiation and management services. In the construction industry Robert has supported clients with contract terms and scope of work crafting, contract negotiations, and document management and control services as well as post-execution contract management including backcharge, warranty, contract close out and dispute resolution. Robert holds advanced degrees in mechanical engineering and is an expert in managing the process of executing commercial transactions from "cradle-to-grave".

Contact Information: robert.mastice@tripower.net

INTRODUCTION

How well business professionals structure contracts and manage risks is an important part of how organizations reduce costs, maximize opportunities and manage risks. The stakes are high. The success of critical commercial transactions depends on flawless execution which in turn requires expert contract management skills. Billions of dollars are spent every year by organizations in procuring goods and services. Even small changes and improvements in how contracts are structured and managed can have substantial positive impacts to the bottom line.

Key questions regarding contract management include:

- How will sound contracting practices, coupled with strong contract management techniques, be part of being successful in an increasingly competitive global environment?

- How will the organization assess, minimize and manage risks in commercial transactions?

- What are the practical steps for standardizing and improving the process of entering into and managing commercial transactions?

Critical success factors for contract management include well defined deliverables, clearly articulated responsibilities, proper administrative controls, training, communication and coordination, tying payment to performance, continuous oversight, protecting rights, preserving leverage and using risk identification and management techniques. This results in lower risks and operating costs.

Although commercial contracts have never been simple, today's transactions have become significantly more complex, with a myriad of technical, commercial and other considerations. Business professionals need to be well versed in the subtleties of how to optimally structure and manage contracts and their associated risks. All too often commercial contracts are entered into with insufficient up-front effort and without a consistent approach or the necessary controls. Today's organizations need to have the systems in place to manage their commercial transactions. This includes ensuring that employees have the skills, strategies and techniques to avoid the pitfalls associated with poor contract management.

It's surprising how many people involved in negotiating and managing contracts know so little about them. There is an old saying that "In History only what is written matters". In many ways this is true when negotiating deals. At the end of the day it's only what makes it into the written contract that you can truly rely on. Moreover, what is written needs to be clear and complete so that ambiguity is eliminated to the greatest extent. This is simple to say but very hard to do in practice. Many things conspire to create confused and ambiguous language in contracts undermining the very purpose of a contract which is certainty and predictability. This book addresses simple and practical steps and techniques to avoid the many "gaps and traps" that tend to make their way into contract documents. Why is this so? Time pressure, false optimism, misplaced trust, inexperience, poor language skills and a variety of other factors conspire to undermine and weaken contract documents.

When asked to say what a contract is the typical business professional will respond "An agreement". This answer only begs the question and falls short of any real understanding. A contract is a legally enforceable promise made up of several components each of which are critical to achieving a contractual obligation. These are: an offer, supported by valuable consideration, followed by acceptance by competent parties for some legal object or purpose. Each of these components have their own legal thresholds and requirements and it's important to understand them all so that the moment when you are contractually bound is actually known. Understanding and controlling the process is key. As buyers business professionals are in the business of collecting offers. The quality of the offers obtained sets the stage for what follows and that is why a controlled Request for Proposals process is so critical. Entering into contracts is easy but making good ones is hard. Nobody always gets a good contract but the key risk and danger is to enter into poor contracts unknowingly or prematurely. Obviously once you are contractually bound you've lost your "walk away" power and any associated leverage.

Entering into and managing contracts is a serious business and should never be done casually or informally. Ill-conceived "hand-shake" deals and premature letters of intent are the antithesis of good contracting since the devil is in the details. Short circuiting the hard work of hammering out the details undermines the whole process. A house built without a good foundation cannot stand and so it is with contracts. Documents which are vague, ambiguous and full of exceptions, qualifications, assumptions or clarifications will come back to haunt the author. Perhaps the clearest example of this is where significant aspects of the deal are left to "future agreement". Poorly articulated workscopes and ill-defined respective responsibilities likewise undermine good contracting. It may be tempting to assume that "it's understood" or "this deal is going to be just like the last one" but this is rarely the case. This book highlights the many typical "gotchas that get you" and ways to avoid them.

FUNDAMENTAL CONCEPTS

Privity of Contract

Privity of contract ("Privity") answers the question of "Who do I have a deal with?" and "Who can I hold accountable?". In essence, which person or entity can you sue if necessary. Who you can hold accountable determines whether you have any real rights and an effective remedy if things go bad.

It is absolutely crucial for anyone involved in contracting, whether at the negotiation stage or after the agreement is signed, to understand the principle of Privity. Simply put, Privity means that the contract, including all the rights, liabilities and responsibilities contained in the contract, only apply to the named parties or specified beneficiaries. Why is this so important? For several reasons.

First and foremost, only the named parties (or specified beneficiaries; something we'll address later) can sue or have any rights and remedies under the agreement. Therefore if you contract with a person or entity that has no cash or assets you may have no effective remedy in the event of a breach or failure to perform. Note that many organizations create legal entities such as corporations, joint ventures or limited liability companies simply to avoid risk by limiting the other parties' ability to recover in the event of a claim or suit. This is not illegal but a risk to be on the lookout for.

For example, Giant XYZ Corporation could form a legal entity in the form of a subsidiary called Giant XYZ Corporation, USA, LLC. That subsidiary would in effect be a separate legal entity or "person" in the eyes of the law with its separate identity, tax payer ID number and independent status. In the event the subsidiary breached its contractual obligations, the parent would generally not be liable. By analogy, if you contract with someone's son or daughter and they don't perform and don't carry out their obligations, you can't sue and recover from the parent. The same is true for business entities.

Essentially, corporate or company liability is limited liability. Even partnerships may have one general partner (which could be a person or legal entity) with very limited assets or resources thereby shielding the limited partners from liability in the event of a breach. This is why it is so crucial for risk managers, business professionals and others involved in contracting to understand the all-important principle of "Privity of Contract". In rare cases it is possible to "pierce the corporate veil" and get to the parent but that can be difficult and expensive. It usually requires some sort of fraudulent behavior or "alter ego" status.

Privity of Contract is something to bear in mind at all phases of the transaction but it is especially important in the early negotiation and contact formation. Early on in the process do your due diligence and understand who in effect you are going to have a binding agreement with in the form of a contract and make sure that person has the deep pockets or resources to honor their commitments including any warranties or indemnities promised under the contract. We will discuss in a bit how to protect yourself in the event that you need or want to do business with an entity that has limited resources. At the outset the key is to understand who you are doing business with, what their resources and capabilities are, and not assume that if they don't perform you can sue the parent just because they have a similar name. Remember, corporations or other entities sometimes form subsidiaries (and as noted sometimes enter into joint ventures or partnerships) to limit their liability.

Another reason to have a full and complete understanding of Privity of Contract concerns how the transaction is managed after the contract is signed. It may be tempting if things aren't going well to go directly to the contractor's or supplier's sub-contractor(s) or sub-supplier(s) (Subs). Since you have no contract with the sub-contractor(s) or sub-supplier(s) you are not in "Privity of Contract" and you have no right to direct or otherwise tell them what to do or how to do what they are doing. You must respect Privity of Contract by going to the contractor or supplier with whom you have a contract and demanding conforming performance from them directly. Because of Privity of Contract, you can't sue the sub-contractor(s) or sub-supplier(s) if they don't perform, but instead your right is to hold the contractor or supplier, as the case may be, accountable for the performance of their Subs.

By the same token, the Subs have no contractual right against you for payment and the last thing you ever want to do is make direct or implied promises to the Subs that if the contractor or supplier, with whom they have a contract, doesn't pay them you will. Directing or promising payment to subs will create mischief in at least two ways. First, the contractor or supplier will claim interference and be provided with an argument against being held accountable. Second, the subs may take your commands or promises and attempt to argue that they create a contractual commitment between you and them. Since you are paying the contractor or supplier for a result and to manage the subs, this is the last thing that you ever want to have happen.

Bear in mind you can be in Privity of Contract with more than one contractor at a time on a particular project. This is called being in a multi-prime arrangement. Obviously there is more to manage when you have multiple prime contractors, all of whom are in Privity of Contract with you. By contrast, a single prime arrangement gives you a single point of accountability.

Apparent Authority

As noted, good contract management begins with good self-management. This means avoiding the apparent authority trap where an employee acts as if he or she had authority but actually doesn't. Everyone involved in a contract, project or working at a site has to understand this risk. It's not unusual for new, "eager beaver" employees to want to "take charge" and start directing everyone and anyone, including subs. This again would be inconsistent with the principle of "Privity of Contract" and could create apparent authority problems. The solution to this is simple, educate your employees including those who are new or with "one year of experience thirty times". Essentially, Apparent Authority can occur when you let people in your organization act as if they have authority to make or modify the contract. If that happens you've lost control of change management, a key to good contract management (See Chapter "Key Contact Management Practices" section 68 entitled "Apparent Authority").

There are rare instances where some communication with the Subs is desirable. It may be that you as the purchaser or owner have a better understanding of a situation and can better explain a problem or challenge better than the contractor or supplier could. The solution here is simple, have the discussion and dialogue with both the contractor or supplier and the respective sub altogether at the same time in the same room. Make it clear all the while that it's the contractor's or supplier's responsibility to get this done and that he or she is responsible for the Subs performance. This way you stay on the right side of Privity of Contract and avoid the Apparent Authority trap.

It's true that some states give Subs certain statutory lien rights under certain conditions but that's a different topic and doesn't change the basic premise of honoring Privity of Contract and avoiding the apparent authority trap. Depending upon the jurisdiction, a well-crafted contract could impose on the contractor or supplier the duty to discharge any such liens. Again, regardless of any applicable local lien laws it is critical to understand and respect Privity and avoid apparent authority as part of any good contract formation and management. The principle of Privity of Contract has been relaxed in certain jurisdictions to allow a third party beneficiary or other foreseeable user to sue the seller of a defective product under a theory of strict liability. In addition, if a contract names a particular person or entity as a beneficiary (i.e. a named third party beneficiary) that person or entity may have a right to sue. These exceptions do not detract from the importance of understanding and applying the principle of Privity but make apparent authority an even more dangerous trap. Of course just because someone may have an incidental or indirect benefit from a contract doesn't make that person an intended beneficiary.

Ensuring an Effective Remedy

What do you do if the entity you want to do business with has limited financial or other resources? Follow the money and look for a deep-pocket; perhaps do the deal with the parent organization. If it's not possible to do the deal directly with a financially strong entity and they have a financially strong parent, a Parental Guarantee can be obtained from the parent. A Parental Guarantee is essentially a separate formal and legal agreement between you and the parent organization stating that if the parent's subsidiary (or other affiliated organization) fails to perform, the parent will step in and be liable.

Of course, not every organization is blessed with a rich parent. In that case, a letter of credit can be used to guarantee performance. A letter of credit, or LOC, is essentially a promise from a bank that in the event of non-performance, the bank will pay a certain sum to the person who is owed the performance. However, since an LOC is the equivalent of having money in the bank, not every organization can afford to set aside a meaningful sum of money and tie up their capital. In addition, banks also charge a fee for the service of providing a letter of credit. Essentially, the bank is "holding" a sum of money out of the Contractor's account to pay off the LOC if the buyer calls it in because of a breach or other deficiency of performance.

Another option is to use payment and performance bonds. Bonds can be unattractive since they involve a surety (a third party) who, in the event of a breach, has the right to step into the breaching parties' shoes and undertake performance. This almost guarantees that the surety will fight the claim and mount its own attack and counterclaim defending the contractor's or supplier's performance. A surety is different than an insurance company in that they never expect to pay a claim on an actuarial basis. So, you will likely have a nasty fight on your hands if you call in the bond. As in the case of letters of credit the surety imposes a fee for this service.

Whether you use a Parental Guarantee, Letter of Credit or Bond remember that these are all forms of contractual promises with a third party guaranteeing, in varying degrees, the contractor's or supplier's performance. How they're worded is crucial and makes all the difference (see Chapter "Allocating Commercial Risks"). And of course all these options are expensive and may not be available at any price. Moreover, they require heavy legal review and drafting to be effective.

Paying for Performance

If you want or need to do business with a judgment proof entity you may have to assume some risk but mitigate that risk by also: (a) tying payment to performance, coupled with a well-crafted payment schedule and (b) withholding a percentage of payments (e.g. 10%) until final completion or warranty expiration (Retainage). Note that even where parental guarantees, letters of credit or bonds are not available, payment should never get ahead of actual conforming work performed. Pay for performance not promises. Good termination rights as well as the right to increase or decrease the scope of work for an agreed upon price or credit can also help mitigate risk.

Privity, Apparent Authority, and Paying for Performance are mechanisms for assuring a remedy that are not mere abstract concepts reserved for lawyers. They have everyday applicability for all persons involved in buying or selling. Without a basic understanding of these concepts your whole contract management process is at risk.

The Integration Clause

All good contracts end with an integration or Entire Agreement clause. This clause states that the contract is the entire agreement between the parties. The net effect of this clause is to preclude anything that is not included in the agreement, either by expressly being stated or incorporated by reference, from being a part of the deal. Only what is within the so-called "Four Corners" of the agreement is part of the contract.

Why is this important? This is important because even sophisticated buyers may not realize that earlier proposals, RFP responses, presentations, emails, correspondence, offers, statements, promises and the like do not survive if they are not contained within the contract itself.

These types of statements or representations are known as "parole evidence" and can only be used to explain what the parties may have meant in the face of an ambiguity or disagreement. Communications outside of what is contained in the contract documents cannot vary or change what is contained in the contract. Accordingly, if there are important promises contained in certain supplier materials such as brochures or presentations, those specific representations need to be reflected or referenced in the contract.

This is not to say that a supplier's entire proposal or promotional should automatically be included by reference into the final contract. That's because supplier's documents may contain exceptions, qualifications, clarifications or other unfavorable provisions that a buyer might find unacceptable. This is especially true since proposals often go through many iterations and may even incorporate the supplier's terms and conditions by reference creating a conflict with the buyer's terms and conditions.

Documenting the Deal

Much of successful supply chain management is managing contracts. As such, your contracts become your primary risk management tool allocating between the parties both risks and responsibilities. How well these contracts are structured and documented in terms of clarity and completeness is crucial. In essence, contracts are a private law between two parties regarding their transaction. It follows that the transaction is only as good as its documentation and management. Of course, the perfect contract is not yet written and "there are no facts, only interpretations" as the saying goes. Another way of saying this is that no matter how flat you make the pancake there are always two sides but that doesn't mean you don't do everything in your power to avoid ambiguity.

Much has been written about the science of supply chain management and the importance of skillful negotiation. Relatively little is available to the supply chain management practitioner on how to structure and document transactions. Of course knowledge of the business and markets is key but so is the skill of forging that knowledge into not just a "deal" but a contract resulting in certainty, predictability and measurable progress. Far too many contracts are based on assumptions, trust and hope or contain language such as "to be agreed upon" and many times the fruits of well-crafted contracts are lost where the transaction is improperly or carelessly managed. Even a good contract will be useless if it is simply filed and forgotten until a problem arises. All contracts require active management and the more complex the transaction the more time and treasure needs to be budgeted for that management.

Front loading the effort will pay big dividends down the road. It usually starts with collecting conforming offers and controlling the paper flow from the beginning. Controlling what is written begins at a very early stage and goes beyond well-defined scopes of work and proper incorporation by reference techniques. Don't fall into the trap of letting the other guy write the contract and keep very tight control over iterations and versions as the negotiations proceed. Version control can be tedious but it is simple. When you exchange drafts always work from your clean draft and add acceptable changes to that draft. Never assume that all the agreed upon changes have actually been entered or are reflected in a document the other side sends you. This technique will certainly inconvenience one side or the other but such is life.

Scope is King

The most fertile ground for improving contract documents is the scope of work which defines what is to be done or delivered. Understandably supply chain management professionals recoil at the thought that they are responsible for something so potentially technical and complex. This is especially true for specialized contracts such as construction projects or IT procurements. Accordingly this book provides simple techniques that can be used to improve and manage the creation of workscopes by the appropriate subject matter experts. For example, workscopes can be improved simply by asking the right questions. The reality is that you can be a very qualified subject matter expert and be completely inept at writing workscopes. Why is this? Subject matter experts tend to write in an expository form as if they were trying to convince the reader of something. In addition, workscopes often suffer from multiple authors who each have their own particular style. This leads to lack of uniformity, ambiguity and duplication. Moreover, subject matter experts have a tendency to make assumptions under the misconception that "it's understood". In addition, subject matter experts tend to live in their individual "silo of expertise" and miss the big picture, the seams and interrelationships. For example, subject matter experts will write a scope of work and completely ignore (or redefine) the definitions set forth in the commercial terms and conditions. Knitting it all together in a cohesive manner that takes into account not only the objective to be achieved but the commercial terms and conditions as well is the role of the supply chain management professional.

Apply Project Management Principles

Every significant contract should have its own Contract Management Plan ("CMP"). This plan is an internal document that helps the owner or contractor fulfill its responsibilities by focusing on each party's respective rights and responsibilities and the administrative steps that need to be taken to comply. For example, a clear and specific protocol for providing notices with correct timing is a vital and integral part of any CMP. In addition, each CMP will set out the various roles and responsibilities for certain individuals and provide guidance to those individuals in how to fulfill their respective responsibilities. The CMP also ties specific actions to specific articles and highlights the timelines and due dates set forth in the contract. The CMP helps set forth the process for managing claims and disputes including warranty claims or requests for changes. These changes could range from increases to the scope of work, additional time or compensation and the like.

KEY BEST PRACTICES IN A NUTSHELL

This Book covers a number of best practices including those listed below. How each of these best practices are actually applied to particular transactions will vary with the individual facts and circumstances. All these best practices simply reflect good overall contract management.

1. Control the contracting process "cradle-to-grave".

2. Don't make assumptions or open-ended commitments.

3. Tie payment to measurable performance not promises.

4. Avoid informal, hand-shake, incomplete or side-bar deals.

5. Collect offers-conforming to what you want and your needs.

6. Avoid automatic renewals and artificial pricing mechanisms.

7. Control the moment of agreement when you are contractually bound.

8. Develop clear and complete scope of work and respective responsibilities.

9. Anticipate changing needs or relationships and how change or transitions will be handled.

10. Build change management into the deal with appropriate cost adjustments for increases or decreases in scope.

11. Capture and apply lessons learned from prior transactions and engage in continuous process improvement and implementation.

12. Apply project management discipline and mentality with kick-offs, well defined and documented reporting requirements and a clear close out process.

CONTRACT MANAGEMENT DEFINED

Contract management is the process by which organizations structure and control their commercial relationships. It requires the accurate assessment of the organization's needs and objectives coupled with a consistent and predictable process for entering into and managing contracts.

There is no one ideal universal contract management model. However, all sound contract management shares certain common characteristics. These characteristics include the ability to:

1. Determine the organization's needs and objectives
2. Create contracts that meet these needs and objectives
3. Continuously train employees and improve the process
4. Monitor, measure and manage contract performance and close out
5. Use the experience and information obtained during the process

Thus, contract management is the "cradle-to-grave" process by which organizations assess needs, negotiate and create contracts, manage the transactions to ensure that responsibilities are fulfilled and utilize the collective corporate experience to the organization's maximum advantage.

Just as there are certain universal characteristics common to sound contract management processes, poor contract management is marked by the following:

1. Repeating past mistakes or shortcomings
2. Inadequate risk identification and assessment
3. Failure to define the parties' respective responsibilities
4. Entering into informal, partial or incomplete agreements
5. Lack of clear delegation of authority or written procedures

The importance of consistency and predictability in the contract management process cannot be over-emphasized. The best practice is to have clearly defined written procedures governing the process for entering into and managing commercial transactions with special emphasis on which few and select individuals have the actual authority to commit the organization.

CONTRACT MANAGEMENT IN A "NUTSHELL"

Contract management is a complex process requiring knowledge, skill, and "art". Those involved in the process should understand the need to:

1. Define the partys' respective responsibilities. (scope of work)

2. Understand contract privity and the "relationship architecture".

3. Assess the counterparty's character, capability, creditworthiness.

4. Vigorously test all assumptions. ("Just like the last project/deal?")

5. Avoid preliminary or incomplete agreements (letters of intent, future mutual agreement, starting work without a contract, or handshake deals premised upon "They know what I mean" or "It's understood").

6. Uphold integrity and guard against the "apparent authority" trap.

7. Anticipate the need for changes and avoid informal changes.

8. Pay for performance by tying payment to actual verified progress.

9. Incorporate the right documents into the contract by reference.

10. Understand the integration clause and parole evidence rule.

11. Get the right financial protection and guarantees. (retention, parental guaranty, letter of credit, or payment and performance bonds on your form)

12. Establish a single point of contact to discourage "forum shopping".

13. Protect what is proprietary, confidential or privileged.

14. Ensure that original contracts are available and signed by all parties.

THE CONTRACT MANAGEMENT BASICS

Contract management basics include the following:

1. Know what you want and be clear about it.

2. Carefully control the following two critical points:

   a) The point of agreement.

   b) The point of acceptance.

3. Preserve your negotiating power and leverage.

4. Remember that the contract will be interpreted according to:

   a) By its terms

   b) What was/is done.

   c) What was/is said.

5. Do not agree to or sign what you have not read.

6. Do not agree to or sign what you do not understand.

7. Do not do verbal or "handshake" deals - get it in writing.

8. Identify what can go wrong and what will happen if it does.

9. Expect and plan for the inevitable change(s) and end.

10. Begin with the end in mind.

11. Understand that "Get it done" means "Get it done RIGHT".

12. Remember that "Scope is king".

CONTRACTS DEFINED

The Layman's Definition: What we say or do.

The Entrepreneur's Definition: An allocation of risk.

The Lawyer's Definition: An offer followed by acceptance supported by valuable consideration between legally competent parties for some legal objective or purpose.

The Elements of A Contract

- Was an offer made?

- Was the offer accepted?

- Is there valuable consideration?

- Are the parties legally competent to contract?

- Is the contract for a legal objective or purpose?

In order for an offer to be capable of acceptance it must be sufficiently detailed and complete so that acceptance will create an agreement. In addition, it is often difficult to determine whether an offer has been accepted given that agreement is typically reached in serial fashion. Understand that the term "valuable consideration" simply means something of value which can be a token amount, a promise to do something or even a promise not to do something. Likewise, the term "legally competent" doesn't mean evenly matched or even smart. Usually, anyone over the age of 18 is "legally competent". Of course you can't enforce a contract that violates the law.

Contract Formation

The law recognizes that when it comes to whether a contract has been made (a meeting of the minds), how you act or what you do is often as relevant as what you say or write. Basically, a contract may be made in any manner sufficient to show agreement. A party is bound by his or her apparent intention as manifested (objective intent), not some hidden secret or subjective intent. The objective intent can be determined by words, writings, or conduct.

A contract can exist even if the moment when it was made is not known. Moreover, parties need not have agreed on every aspect of their bargain before an enforceable contract is reached. Of course, the greater the number of "open terms", the less likely a contract has been made. In addition, parties can agree that they will not be contractually obligated unless and until a contract is signed or that any contractual commitment is subject to some contingency such as higher approval.

A contract can best be defined by its purpose, namely to reduce uncertainty and increase predictability. The world is full of risks including the risk of violating laws, destroying reputation, losing or violating intellectual property rights or damage to operations. A well-conceived and well-constructed contract which both parties sign together with good contract management is the key to success. Since purchase orders are typically unsigned and not tailored, they can be problematic. The trade-off is convenience and simplicity versus predictability and certainty. Although an exchange of forms can create a contract, inconsistencies or contradictions between the buyer and seller's forms (the classic "battle of the forms") creates ambiguity and uncertainty. The key to winning the battle of the forms is not to fight the battle but instead use carefully constructed and tailored contracts for all significant or high risk transactions.

THE FOUR R'S OF CONTRACTS:
RISKS, RIGHTS, RESPONSIBILITIES, AND RESOURCES

How To Evaluate Commercial Transactions

All commercial transactions can be evaluated in terms of the following:

- Risks

- Rights

- Responsibilities

- Resources

The Four Key Questions To Ask

- What are the associated RISKS?

- What are the parties' respective RIGHTS?

- What are the parties' respective RESPONSIBILITIES?

- Does each of the parties have the necessary RESOURCES to do the job in terms of capability, capital, and character?

The relationship between risk and rights, responsibilities, and resources

- The greater your rights, the lower your risk.

- The fewer your responsibilities, the lower your risk.

- The more resources the other party has, the lower your risk.

- The greater the risks, the more resources needed.

THE IMPORTANCE OF TERMINOLOGY

Some of the key terms that contract managers need to know include those listed below. The definitions provided below are for discussion purposes only and are not a complete or comprehensive listing of terms or their meanings.

ACCEPTANCE – The point at which goods or services are accepted. Note that acceptance can be qualified or under a reservation of rights.

AGREEMENT – The point at which a "meeting of the minds" occurs, objectively judged which satisfies the elements of a contract.

AUTHORITY – An agent's power to bind or commit the principal. Authority can be actual, apparent, or implied which can all be binding. The existence and scope of authority is critical.

CONFIDENTIAL INFORMATION – Information which is not generally known and which is not disclosed except to a select group under specific restrictions.

COPYRIGHTS – Author's exclusive rights, created by statute, which prevent the reproduction, distribution or display of "expressions" including music, writings, pictures, recordings, designs or sculptures which are original works.

DAMAGES – Typically financial consideration, whether direct, consequential, liquidated, incidental or otherwise, for breach of a contract.

ENTIRE AGREEMENT OR INTEGRATION CLAUSE – Specifies the entire complete and only agreement between the parties.

FIRM OFFER – Creates the power of acceptance, but is not revocable during the time specified. Under the UCC, a merchant's written signed assurance that the offer will be held open is not revocable for the period stated (or if none stated, for a reasonable time), not to exceed three months.

FORCE MAJEURE – An event excusing performance as defined or provided by the contract. Generally, Force Majeure should not excuse performance where the event was foreseeable or controllable. Nor should Force Majeure excuse performance where the event was due to an act of neglect by the party seeking relief or such party's failure to minimize and mitigate any impacts.

GOOD FAITH – The obligation contained in every contract to be honest and give the other party the benefit of its bargain. Bad faith in contracts deals with dishonest behavior but it is not bad faith to exercise one's rights, hold the other party to the bargain or take advantage of a good deal.

NOTICE – A communication which is often a contractual or legal requirement as a condition of receiving a remedy under the contract. Contracts often specify that specific events require written notice to one or more designated individuals.

MATERIALS - Any articles, apparatus, goods, materials, products, items, data, documents, supplies, equipment, component parts and assemblies, or any other substances, parts, or any combination thereof used, consumed, furnished or installed by the Contractor or its Subcontractors under the Contract.

OFFER – That which creates the power of acceptance, but is usually revocable at will any time prior to acceptance.

OPTION – Creates a right but not the obligation to exercise that right. An option is a contract (or part of a contract) and must be supported by consideration. Unlike a firm offer, an option requires separate consideration and can be for any length of stated time.

PAROL EVIDENCE – Extrinsic evidence (words or conduct) used to explain but not vary the terms of the contract.

PATENTS – Rights created by statute which prevent the manufacture, use, or sale of "inventions", including processes, designs, and plants, without the inventor's consent.

PRIVITY – The parties to the contract are said to be in "privity". Privity defines the individuals or entities who are bound under the contract.

PROOF – Evidence which supports a position which can include business records, photographs, eyewitness testimony, expert opinion, admissions and the like.

PURCHASE ORDER - The document including the order number which is generated by the Company's accounting system following Contract execution and which will be used for payment administration purposes.

RIGHT OF FIRST REFUSAL – Creates the right to be given the opportunity to make a purchase or sale at some stipulated price should the other party elect to buy or sell, but does not give the holder the power to compel the other party to buy or sell. Conversely, the holder is not compelled to buy or sell.

TRADE SECRETS – Rights created by statute and common law which protect "secrets" consisting of valuable information which gives the owner a competitive advantage which can include customer lists, plans, forecasts and business methods.

VENUE AND CHOICE OF LAW – Where disputes will be resolved and the law which will be applied.

WAIVER AND ESTOPPEL – Are legal and equitable which can be used to lose contract rights or remedies. A waiver is the intentional and voluntary act of giving up a known right. Estoppel provides a remedy for reasonably relying, to one's detriment, on words or acts. Estoppel can be based either on words (promissory estoppel) or conduct (equitable estoppel).

WARRANTY – Are promises, whether express or implied, made as part of the bargain for which there is a remedy. Generally, implied warranties such as "merchantability" or "fitness of goods for a particular purpose" can be disclaimed.

WORK - Any labor, supervision, technical advice, work direction, design, testing, inspection, engineering support, or services or Materials provided by Contractor or Subcontractors to the Company under the Contract. The word "Work" specifically includes "Materials" as defined in the Contract.

WRITTEN NOTICE - A written communication signed by a duly authorized representative and delivered in accordance with the Contract.

THE CONTRACTING PROCESS

Entering into commercial transactions typically involves these steps:

1. Determine the need(s).

2. Define the deliverable(s).

3. Develop options and alternatives.

4. Anticipate changing requirements.

5. Anticipate increases or decreases in price(s).

6. Anticipate technological progress/obsolescence.

7. Anticipate cancellation and termination.

8. Anticipate disputes and disagreements.

9. Identify and assess the associated risks.

10. Know and control the moment of agreement.

11. Protect and preserve confidential information.

12. Ensure that all contract documents have been read.

13. Ensure that all contract documents are understood.

14. Memorialize agreement and any amendments.

15. Manage and administer the agreement.

TEN QUESTIONS REGARDING CONTRACTS

Everyone thinks they know what a contract is but it's always good to remind oneself as to the components and timing that make up a contract.

1. What is a contract?
   [Short answer: A legally enforceable promise.]

2. What is the purpose of a contract?
   [Short answer: To allocate risk and responsibility.]

3. When do we have a contract?
   [Short answer: When we agree or act like we do.]

4. What does the contract consist of?
   [Short answer: What we say and do.]

5. When is a writing a legal requirement?
   [Short answer: Rarely, but always desirable.]

6. Who has authority to contract?
   [Short answer: Persons with actual or apparent authority.]

7. What contract terms are indispensable?
    [Short answer: Only quantity.]

8. How can the contract be changed?
    [Short answer: By words or conduct.]

9. What are the risks of a contract?
    [Short answer: Breach and resulting damages.]

10. What if the agreement is ambiguous?
    [Short answer: Look to words and conduct.]

GENERAL PRINCIPLES APPLICABLE TO CONTRACTS

People tend to think of contracts as a lot of complicated words written in fine print that nobody ever needs to read. The tendency is to ignore the contract and instead rely on personal relationship and a subjective view of what the parties meant. All good contract managers know and understand that all commercial transactions are essentially contractual, not personal, in nature.

The importance of the legal terms and conditions contained in any agreement cannot be ignored. However, understand that a contract's "boiler plate" may not be the most critical part of success. It may be as or more productive to spend time and effort on defining the parties' respective responsibilities, structuring the payment provisions, defining the test or acceptance criteria, and setting the schedule or deadlines for delivery or performance.

Notwithstanding the fact that commercial transactions are legal relationships governed by the contract and the law, the following general principles are easily understood by non-lawyers.

1. Contracts Are Easy To Make.

Contractual commitments are easily made. Essentially, an offer followed by acceptance creates a contract. Of course, the contract has to be for a legal purpose, the parties must be legally competent, and the deal has to be supported by valuable consideration, typically money or a promise. However, no special or magic words are needed. Hence the need to control the moment of agreement.

2. You Can Agree To Almost Anything.

Free enterprise is premised on freedom of contract. A contract is basically a private "law" between the parties. Naturally, the parties cannot contract to act illegally. For example, an agreement to injure a third person would be illegal and unenforceable. But the parties are free to make just about any deal, good or bad, they wish. No judge or jury is going to help you out just because you made a bad deal.

3. You Can Set Conditions.

You can make an offer or contract conditional. For example, you can agree that any contract is subject to higher approval, the execution of a formal document by duly authorized agents, or some contingency. You can also agree that no claims will be filed unless proper notices are filed or certain information is provided.

4. You Can Limit Liability.

You can agree that a party's liability under a contract will be limited to a set amount or specific obligation. For example, some contracts contain a limited warranty, specified (liquidated) damages in the event of a breach or an exclusion for consequential loss or damage.

5. You Can Shift Liability.

A contract can reflect the parties' intent to allocate or shift liability. Generally, a party is free to accept the risks of unanticipated conditions, unforeseen circumstances, injury, loss, or damage. A contract is essentially an agreement on who has what risks and responsibilities.

6. Contracts Can Be Changed.

Parties can always agree to change a contract or enter into a new contract. However, a contract can also be changed by conduct or by intentionally giving up (waiving) contract rights. Where a party reasonably relies on the other parties' conduct or statements, the law may stop (estop), the other party from asserting his or her rights. However, unless provided for in the agreement, there is no automatic right to change the contract. The key is to include good change management provisions in your contract and guard against unintentional changes.

7. Breach Results In Damages.

The law follows a "make whole" approach to contract violations. The standard remedy for breach of contract is payment for damages the amount of money needed to compensate the non-breaching party for his or her losses. Compensatory damages include both direct and consequential losses such as lost profits or increased costs. Generally, punitive damages are not available in breach of contract cases. Of course, despite a breach, damages must still be proved and not all breaches necessarily result in recoverable damages.

8. Contract Liability Is Strict.

The law requires that contracts be strictly adhered to. Generally, there are very few excuses for not performing. For example, just because something turns out to be more difficult or expensive to perform does not excuse a contract to do it. Neither do errors in judgment. Unilateral mistakes of fact, likewise, do not usually excuse performance. People are free to make bad contracts as long as there is no fraud or bad faith involved.

9. No Automatic Right To Terminate.

A contract is a commitment, and there is no automatic right to terminate (or even change) the agreement. Of course, the parties can agree to specified termination rights or that one party has the right to end or change (e.g., order extras) the agreement.

10. Vagueness Does Not Preclude Enforceability.

All terms and conditions need not be agreed to or specified to have a legally enforceable contract. As long as the parties agree on quantity and indicate an intent to be bound, the law can fill in the gaps by implying a reasonable price, delivery date, warranty, and the like.

TEN KEY CONSIDERATIONS APPLICABLE TO COMMERCIAL TRANSACTIONS

What follows is a list of some of the key considerations applicable to contracts. Keeping these in mind will help you structure your thinking.

1. <u>Scope</u>. Are the parties' respective responsibilities and obligations clearly and completely spelled out in the agreement?

2. <u>Risks</u>. Have the risks associated with the transaction been identified and allocated in the agreement?

3. <u>Warranties</u>. Are the parties' respective warranties, obligations, and remedies spelled out in the agreement?

4. <u>Liability</u>. Does the agreement contain appropriate limitations of liability and damage exclusions?

5. <u>Changes and Waivers</u>. Does the agreement contain appropriate provisions regarding changes, amendments, and waivers?

6. <u>Law and Forum</u>. Does the agreement reflect the parties' choice of law and where any disputes will be litigated?

7. <u>Notice</u>. Does the agreement contain appropriate notice provisions in the event of claims or breach?

8. <u>Limitations Period</u>. Does the agreement set the applicable limitations period by which any claims must be made?

9. <u>Termination</u>. Does the agreement contain appropriate termination for convenience or cause provisions?

10. <u>Integration and Incorporation</u>. Does the agreement specify that it contains the parties' entire final agreement and does the contract incorporate all and only the correct documents?

THE IMPORTANCE OF THE "FIRST STEP"

"A good beginning makes for a good ending", as the old saying goes. From a buyer's perspective it all begins with collecting offers. Why is this so important? Offers empower and provide choices and options. Moreover, offers do not commit the person receiving them to any course of action until they are accepted.

The elements of the contracting process (an offer followed by acceptance supported by valuable consideration for a legal object or purpose by competent parties), typically begin with receiving proposals from contractors or suppliers. For reasons which will become clear, how proposals (i.e. in effect, offers) are solicited is crucial. If your request for proposal (RFP) process is not structured in a way to yield conforming and responsive offers, you're off to a bad start. As in the case of a Moon shot being off by a few degrees when your rocket leaves the earth will cause you to miss the Moon by a mile. Thus, the RFP process needs to be structured and controlled.

Even with the best of controls the RFP process may yield uncertain responses. Many times proposals contain objectionable materials that really don't respond to your needs. Proposals full of exceptions, assumptions, clarifications and the like essentially contain poisonous and sometimes fatal "pills". For example, it's not unusual for proposals to basically attempt to sell what a contractor or supplier has available instead of what the purchaser really needs. This is just human nature but a tendency that needs to be guarded against. In addition, proposals may contain, or incorporate by reference, unacceptable risk shifting or even unfavorable commercial terms and conditions. This is why it is unwise to uniformly and routinely include proposals in the final contract documents. Instead, proposals should be collected from various sources and used to craft appropriate work scopes.

If you think about it, a proposal is written in the form of an offer. Offer type language doesn't belong in a contract since the contract represents not just the offer but the deal. Generally, contracts are divided into two basic components, namely: (1) The Scope of Work detailing the results to be achieved or the deliverables to be provided, and (2) the commercial terms and conditions which reflect risk allocation, warranties, indemnities, insurance, schedule, price and the like.

Essentially you want to solicit offers that are firm for a period of time to allow you to negotiate the best deal possible by looking at all the possibilities and options reasonably available to you. Don't confuse offers (i.e. proposals) with carefully crafted scope of work documents written from your perspective and reflecting your needs. Crafting a good scope of work is the next critical step after collection responsive offers.

The importance of "the first step" is also underscored in the decision by the supply chain management professional regarding whether to use a purchase order or formal contract to document the transaction. Aside from poor workscopes, the inappropriate use of purchase orders is rampant. Essentially a purchase order is a method of contracting created by the Uniform Commercial Code (as that code has been adopted by individual States) applicable to the purchase of goods. Using a purchase order to purchase services is asking for trouble. Purchase orders are intended to be used where scope is almost irrelevant since mass produced goods are being purchased. As long as you've got the make and model number and your purchase order contains appropriate commercial terms they are safe to use. Their ease of use is both their greatest strength and greatest weakness. However, high-risk transactions including those involving services do not lend themselves to purchase orders. Where scope, schedule and compensation terms are complex and detailed the traditional form of contracting requiring both parties to sign a well-crafted agreement is preferred.

RFQS, RFIS AND RFPS COMPARED AND CONTRASTED

1. <u>RFQs, RFIs and RFPs:</u> are part of the overall process which includes;

   - Planning the deal
   - Planning the selection process
   - The solicitation/bid request phase
   - The decision and final selection phase
   - The contract negotiation/formation phase
   - Administration/management of the contract
   - Termination/close-out of the contract at the end

2. <u>Acronyms:</u> be clear with your intent since these terms are definitional.

   - RFQ - "Request for Quote" means "quote me a price"
   - RFI - "Request for Information" means "give me information"
   - RFP - "Request for Proposal" means "make me a bid/offer"

3. <u>Objectives:</u> collect information, obtain pricing data, facilitate decision-making and selection, empower buyer to accept/reject legally binding offers.

4. <u>Preparation:</u> takes time/effort and;

- A disciplined approach
- Everyone gets their say
- Forces team to focus on priorities
- Forces team to address tough questions early
- What kind of contract is contemplated: resources or results?
- A team effort – purchasing/technical/legal/end users/clients
- Will the contract have a "specification standard", a "performance standard" or a mixture of both, e.g. product/system must" (1) meet xyz standards/size and (2) be able to ….".

5. <u>Standards:</u> Be careful when setting standards – Too high or low can have adverse consequences.

6. <u>Results vs. Resources:</u> Ideally, define deliverable as a "result" – what supplier/contract or is to achieve.

7. <u>Acceptance:</u> A big point in the life of the contract.

- How do you know the "performance" has been met – define acceptance, test/ criteria.
- Note: Buyer's rights/remedies typically change after acceptance.

8. <u>Confidentiality:</u> Protect the integrity of the process.

9. <u>Ownership/Right to Use Information:</u> Will you be constrained?

10. <u>On-site Work?</u> Consider: access, safety, insurance, special terms.

11. <u>Forms and Format:</u> Make them user-friendly.

12. <u>Terms and Conditions</u>: Attach/tailor appropriate set.

13. <u>Information</u>: What and how much to include.

14. <u>Questions from Bidders</u>:

   • Formal contacts only
   • Written Questions only
   • Consider pre-bid meeting

15. <u>Integration</u>: Incorporation by reference and Entire Agreement Provisions. Avoid the "but you said…" trap.

16. <u>Non-conforming/Unacceptable responses</u>

   • Qualified offers "we will substitute…"
   • Incomplete offers "we will only …"
   • Exceptions "we take exception to …"
   • Clarifications "you must mean …"
   • Assumptions "we assume …"
   • Expiring offers "good until …"
   • Conditional offers "if you agree"
   • Poison pills "you must buy…"

17. <u>How to Manage Unacceptable Bids</u>.

   • Have a plan
   • Set rules/expectations
   • Be prepared to reject all bids
   • Define priorities and importance
   • Request "revised"/final proposals

- Protect the integrity of the process

18. Potential Basis of Award and Evaluation Factors

- For "Equipment/Goods" proposals can be evaluated based on:

    1) Quality
    2) Service
    3) Delivery
    4) Support
    5) Price

- For "Projects/Services" proposals can be evaluated based on:

    1) Approach – Quality of approach.

    2) Experience and Expertise – Similar projects or undertakings.

    3) Corporate Compliance – Demonstrated history of responsible corporate behavior, including complying with laws.

    4) Technology and Methodology – Application of proven technology and methods designed for high reliability and efficiency.

    5) Quality – of both team and organization.

    6) Schedule – Shortest demonstrable completion schedule.

    7) Project Execution – Quality and completeness of the execution plan, which must fully demonstrate the ability to deliver.

8) <u>Financial Capability and Creditworthiness</u> – Proposal should be from financially strong, creditworthy entities.

9) <u>Compliance with Scope of Work/Requirements</u> – The bidder must demonstrate a clear understanding and ability to perform.

10) <u>Compliance with Contract Terms and Conditions</u> – Discourage exceptions to the Contract Terms and Conditions.

11) <u>Safety Performance</u> – A corporate commitment to safety and demonstrated strong safety performance on past work.

12) <u>Price Certainty</u> - The proposal must reflect price certainty.

NEGOTIATION

Negotiation will be part of the process from "cradle to grave" and will continue throughout the contract's duration. Negotiation presents the opportunity to learn the facts and resolve issues when leverage is high. Keep the following in mind:

Influencing Skills

There are lots of books and publications on how to negotiate or improve negotiating skills and their contents need not be repeated here. The caveat is that if people believe they are being negotiated with, resistance and suspicion may rise. Perhaps the mind-set should be to apply influencing skills rather than negotiating skills. The distinction is subtle.   Influencing draws on your leadership and coaching behaviors with active listening and effective questioning as your primary tools. The answers to your questions are then repeated and perhaps reshaped to more accurately reflect the true intent of the parties. Of course, information, power, tactics and psychology still play a role but influencing is based on building trust and admiration. People trust others who consistently do what they say they will do when they say they will do it. People also trust and are heavily influenced by people they admire. If you have developed a reputation for honestly and expertise people will more readily be influenced by you. Interestingly, there is some information to suggest that if you enjoy a reputation for integrity and honesty, others are more likely to be truthful with you. You can fancy yourself the best negotiator in the world, but if people don't trust you, you won't be successful. Another key point: people tend to inherently trust their facts and information and distrust the facts and information brought to them by others. So, try to point out how their information actually supports your points of view.

Key Considerations

1. Are commitments enforceable?

2. Do the parties trust each other?

3. What role will time or delay play?

4. What uncertainties do the parties face?

5. What factors, if any, will drive settlement?

6. Could threats influence the negotiations?

7. Can either party "walk away" from the deal?

8. Will there be internal and external negotiations?

9. Does each "side" consist of more than one "party"?

10. Is ratification required by a third person or party?

11. Will there be one issue or many interrelated issues?

12. Will there be linkage to other negotiations or events?

13. Are the negotiations between allies or enemies?

14. Will this be a "one-time" deal or repeat negotiations?

15. If agreement cannot be reached, can third parties play a role?

Negotiation Dynamics

Most people never want to hear the word "No" but good negotiators do. Negotiating depends on figuring out what is critical to your side and being prepared to make concessions. It requires the negotiator to: anticipate a "no deal" scenario, develop options or alternatives, know the "bottom line" (deal breakers), and preserve "walk-away" power. The goal is to reach agreement, avoid ambiguity and create certainty with a clear and complete contract.

Making Concessions

A key consideration in negotiation strategy is the pattern of concessions to be made. Typically, the difference between the offers become successively smaller, thereby indicating that a limit is being approached.

Agency And Authority

When negotiating, the question of authority is crucial. A clear understanding of an agent's authority, whether express, implied, or apparent, is required. Know the limits of your authority and, if possible, that of your adversary.

Hallmarks Of Good Negotiators

The probability of agreement is increased when the negotiators are:

- Well-prepared
- Follow a plan
- Of high rank or status
- Patient and persistent

- In control of their "team"
- Good at communication
- Perceptive and persuasive
- Able to be analyzed quickly

Commitment Breaches

If the opposing side wants to break away from commitments, it may:

- Claim lack of authority

- Add additional new issues

- Claim new marching orders

- Claim new information has been obtained

- Replace the negotiator with another person

Preparing Drafts

Remember that if negotiations are going to revolve around a document, the party that prepares the first draft of the document has the advantage of working from a document that shapes expectations and emphasizes key considerations.

Offers And Acceptance

Remember that negotiations are supposed to lead to an agreement which is, in effect, a contract. An agreement consists of an offer followed by an acceptance. However, an offer can be terminated by rejection or revocation any time prior to acceptance. In addition, an offer can be conditioned upon particular events or otherwise limited. On the other hand, an offer can be made a "firm offer".

Preliminary Agreements

The question of when negotiations ripen into a contractual commitment is a key consideration. Remember that refusal to sign a fully negotiated agreement can be a breach of contract. However, the parties can express the intention not to be bound until the execution of a formal contract.

WHEN DO YOU HAVE AGREEMENT?

Controlling the moment of agreement is a critical part of the contracting process. Since offers empower but do not bind you, collecting offers as part of the contracting process is critical. Preserve your leverage by making it clear that there is no deal and certainly no contract unless and until a formal agreement is formally executed by duly authorized representatives.

It is true that often progress toward an ultimate agreement is made in serial fashion by agreeing to parts of the proposed transaction in a step-by-step process. It is often difficult to determine exactly when agreement has been reached. It is also sometimes tempting to declare success and that agreement has been reached subject to reaching agreement on some aspects of the deal. This is a dangerous way to do business. Understanding when preliminary agreements can bind a party is crucial to good risk management. Generally speaking, its best to avoid the use of preliminary agreements and hold fast to the rule of no deal unless and until a contract is formally executed by both parties.

Letters of Intent (LOIs), Memorandums of Understanding (MOUs), Commitment Letters, Negotiating Memorandum, Meeting minutes, correspondence and the like may all constitute preliminary agreements to which the parties may be contractually bound. The label placed on a preliminary agreement may be an indication of whether the parties intended to be bound, but does not definitively decide the issue.

There are essentially three basic types of situations which may contractually bind the parties. They are as follows:

- The parties have agreed to negotiate in good faith, or use "best efforts to agree" or to negotiate exclusively with one party for some time.

- The parties have agreed to some terms but other terms remain to be negotiated and agreed upon.

- The parties have agreed on all the terms and merely want to formalize the existing unwritten agreement with a formal written contract.

There are four basic factors to consider when considering whether parties intended to be bound in the absence of a final document signed by both sides.

- Have specific terms been agreed upon?
- Has there been part performance of the contract?
- Has there been a reservation of right not to be bound without a formal contract signed by duly authorized representatives for both sides?
- Is the type of agreement at issue usually committed to writing based on past practice, course of conduct or what is usual and customary in the industry?

The risk of entering into a contractually binding preliminary agreement can be avoided or reduced by <u>specifying</u> that:

- It is merely an agreement to try to agree
- It does not create any obligation or liability
- The parties do not intend to be legally bound

and by further specifying that any agreement is <u>contingent</u> upon:

- Future agreement on open terms
- Future approvals by others in authority
- The signing of a final and formal contract

Note that whether the parties intended to be contractually bound is:

- Highly <u>subjective</u>
- Highly <u>fact-sensitive</u>
- Depends on manifestations of <u>intent</u>

Enforcement of preliminary agreements is more likely when there is:

- Detrimental reliance on clear promises
- An objective intent to be contractually bound
- Unjust enrichment by the party seeking to avoid the agreement

WHEN AND HOW TO USE LETTERS OF INTENT

Letters of Intent, and other forms of preliminary agreement, should only be used rarely and carefully since they are the antithesis of a clear and complete contract.

In structuring such ambiguous and uncertain documents, think carefully about how leverage is lost as a result of such preliminary commitments. Consider how to limit this disadvantage. Here are some potential approaches:

1. Limit the obligation to negotiating for some set period of time.

2. If preliminary goods or services are to be provided while negotiations are ongoing, specify that the Company's standard terms and conditions will apply pending agreement upon the definitive contract terms.

3. Require that any goods or services be approved in writing before they are provided.

4. Require that pricing and billing procedures be agreed upon upfront.

Always consider more definitive alternatives to Letter of Intent such as Letter Agreements or Limited Notices to Proceed (LNTP) which can be structured to contain more detailed terms, conditions, schedule, pricing and payment provisions.

IDENTIFYING AND EVALUATING RISKS

An essential purpose of any contract is to allocate the parties' respective rights, risks, and responsibilities. As a general rule, commercial entities are free to allocate the risks arising out of their contractual undertakings as they see fit.

In the context of a commercial contract, the parties may accept, allocate, or shift the risk of both anticipated or unanticipated expenses or difficulties in performing the contract. Commercial entities are also free to exclude the recovery of consequential damages, limit their liability to each other, and disclaim any express or implied warranties.

Generally, where a person enters into a contract to do something for a fixed amount of money, he is not entitled to additional compensation simply because unanticipated difficulties are encountered. It is not the function of a court to rewrite contracts, but instead to interpret them as actually made.

Business persons are free to exercise judgment and take risks. As risk takers, business persons are not usually protected against a loss or guaranteed a profit. However, a careful and studied allocation of the risks provides the parties with predictability and certainty, as well as facilitating the resolution of any disputes.

As noted, sound contract management requires identifying and evaluating the risks, as well as taking steps to eliminate or minimize those risks. The following steps can help in managing risks as part of the contract management process:

1. Identify and make a list of the risks. What are the risks?

2. Evaluate the risks in terms of probability. How likely is it that the risk will occur?

3. Evaluate the risks in terms of their consequences. What are the consequences of taking (or avoiding) the risks?

4. Weight the potential for success against the consequences of failure. Does the potential reward justify the risks?

5. Make a list of ways to manage or control the risks. What can be done contractually or otherwise to eliminate or minimize the risks?

6. Avoid risking a lot to gain a little. Is this a "high-risk, low-gain" transaction with a lot of risk for little gain?

7. Avoid risking more than you can afford to lose. Does the probability of success justify the risks that are being incurred?

8. Identify who is at risk and which party or entity should bear the risk. Is the party at risk able to both control and bear the risk?

9. Determine the duration of the risk. Is the risk "short-term" or "long-term" and does taking the risk have potential long-term consequences?

10. Manage and control the risk. Can the transaction be structured and administered so as to maximize "high-reward, low-risk" potential?

Remember that risk management is everyone's job and good contracts and contract management procedures are a key factor in risk management.

It is often difficult to determine what is a "high-risk" transaction. In addition, it is often difficult to determine "when" to obtain subject matter expert review and input. Below is a list of what are often considered to be "high-risk" transactions meriting careful crafting and review of their associated contracts:

1. Transactions involving "new ventures";

2. Transaction involving joint purchases;

3. Transactions involving "first of a kind" goods or services;

4. Transactions posing a high potential for environmental impacts;

5. Transactions involving parties located in different countries;

6. Transactions presenting technological or other obsolescence risk;

7. Transactions with regulatory and governmental bodies or entities;

8. Transactions with a high potential for consequential loss or damage;

9. Transactions with inexperienced or first time suppliers;

10. Transactions with long-term commitments;

11. Transactions which cannot be terminated easily; or,

12. Transactions where valuable intellectual property rights (licenses, patents, copyrights, trade secrets) are involved.

The second step in this process is to address "when" subject matter experts should be involved. There are two (2) components to this question. The first component pertains to the qualitative aspect of the question, i.e. which transactions should be reviewed by the appropriate subject matter expert(s). The second component pertains to the temporal aspect of the question, i.e. the timing. Individual organizations will have their own rules depending upon the facts, circumstances and nature of the transaction. Typically, the subject matter experts involved would include the following:

A. Legal Review:

Typically this involves a numeric threshold as well as "high-risk" transactions.

B. Credit Review:

Risk management typically provides for input and review by subject matter experts depending upon certain thresholds or triggers.

C. Accounting and Tax Review:

If a transaction exceeds certain dollar thresholds and contains non-standard agreement terms and conditions accounting and tax review is typically triggered.

SAMPLE RISKS AND ALLOCATION TECHNIQUES

The following risk allocation techniques can be used to manage or mitigate certain risks. Some of the techniques will require input from insurance experts, attorneys or other subject matter experts.

1. Needs may change.
   •Changes clause •Termination clause

2. Costs or prices may change.
   •Escalation clause •Price warranty •Termination clause

3. Circumstances or events may change.
   •Force majeure clause •Termination clause

4. Delays may occur.
   •Time of the essence clause •No damage clause •LD's

5. Insolvency may occur.
   •Guarantee clause •Due diligence
   •Identification, segregation, and access clauses

6. Breach or violation may occur.
   •Termination clause •Indemnity clause •Warranty clause

7. Mistakes or errors may be made.
   •Disclaimer clause •Warranty •Insurance

8. Key personnel or subcontractors may leave or change.
   •Termination clause •Approval clause •Specified team

9. Laws or regulations may be violated.
   •Indemnity clause •Insurance •Oversight

10. Injury, loss, or damage may occur.
    •Indemnity clause •Insurance clause •Risk of loss in transit clause

11. Implied changes may occur.
    •Changes clause •Notice provisions •Non-waiver clauses

12. Lawsuits or claims may occur.
    •Choice of law •Choice of venue •Limitations clause

RANKING RISK MANAGEMENT TECHNIQUES

Each transaction will be different and have a different risk ranking profile. Rank (1 through 15) the following risk management techniques in their order of relative importance depending on the particular transaction. This should help you manage your risks.

A. _____ Make a careful selection of vendor/contractor.

B. _____ Control the moment when contractually bound.

C. _____ Carefully inspect all deliverables prior to acceptance.

D. _____ Give prompt notice of any breach of contract.

E. _____ Confirm all important matters in writing.

F. _____ Respond to correspondence promptly and accurately.

G. _____ Carefully and completely identify and allocate risks.

H. _____ Do not become infatuated with a particular vendor.

I. _____ Maintain the integrity of the process.

J. _____ Use contractual techniques to limit liability.

K. _____ Avoid waiving contractual rights or remedies.

L. _____ Avoid making inadvertent promises or commitments.

M. _____ Monitor contract performance to ensure compliance.

N. _____ Seek appropriate and timely legal guidance.

O. _____ Use appropriate insurance coverages

TYPICAL RISKS (BREACHES)

Every commercial transaction runs risks including:

1. The wrong deliverables arrive.

2. The vendor falls behind schedule.

3. The deliverables arrive late (late show).

4. The deliverables provided are defective.

5. The vendor tells you it will not perform.

6. The deliverables never arrive (no show).

7. The warranty efforts are not successful.

8. The vendor fails to pay its subs or suppliers.

9. The vendor fails to provide adequate assurances.

10. The warranty (e.g., repair, replace, reperform, refund) is not honored.

<u>Good contract management anticipates that such problems may occur. Have a plan (or at least some rights and remedies in your contract) for dealing with such situations.</u>

IDENTIFYING "HIGH RISK" TRANSACTIONS

Certain commercial transactions require the exercise of heightened risk management skills. Identifying which transactions are potentially risky is not always easy. The following is a list of potentially "high risk" deals:

1. Deals involving "new ventures"

2. Deals for prototypical "first of a kind" items

3. Deals with high potential for environmental impacts

4. Deals with poorly financed or highly leveraged entities

5. Deals predicated on letters of intent or future agreement

6. Deals where the parties are located in different countries

7. Deals with a poorly defined Scope or Statement of Work

8. Deals where technological or other obsolescence is a risk

9. Deals with regulatory and governmental bodies or entities

10. Deals with high potential for consequential loss or damage

11. Deals with entities who have not previously worked together

12. Deals with long-term commitments without the option to terminate

13. "First time" deals for purchase or sale of a particular item or service

14. Deals between entities that are different or incompatible

15. Deals where valuable intellectual property rights (patents, copyrights, trade secrets) will be created or exchanged

ALLOCATING COMMERCIAL RISKS

When hiring a contractor or supplier there are three key factors to consider: "character, capability and creditworthiness". The term "creditworthiness" is a subjective judgment about a counter-party's financial ability to fulfill its contractual obligations. When evaluating this financial ability numerous factors play a role including:

1. Selecting a qualified contractor with expertise and experience.

2. Securing adequate contractual rights and remedies including the right to: terminate, suspend, demand adequate assurances of performance, obtain status and schedule data, increase or decrease the scope of work, withhold payments, set off any claims against amounts owed, retainage, required invoice documentation, hold payments until due, insurance coverage, as well as securing credit guarantees such as letters of credit or parental guarantees.

3. As noted above, there are many ways to protect one's interests when dealing with the counter-party. These include:

a. Making a careful selection

b. Tying payment to performance

c. Retaining a percentage of money from payments due until final completion

d. Favorable commercial terms and conditions

e. A parent guarantee as appropriate if available

f. A letter of credit as appropriate if available

g. Judicious use of payment and performance bonds

4. Fundamentally, good risk managers seek an appropriate level of protection and predictability given the nature of the particular transaction. Bear in mind that letters of credit or bonds have a cost which is borne by the Company either directly or indirectly.

5. Every transaction has risk and the level of that risk will depend on many factors including the amount of competition, the respective leverage the parties have and the relative need for the goods/services involved. The acceptability of a particular transaction needs to be judged holistically given all of the facts.

Review and Approvals

Every organization should have its particular, well defined process for reviewing risk as well as the requisite specified approvals.

Steps for Assessing Financial Status

Review industry rating reports.
Obtain publicly available information.
Evaluate whether information available suggests a risk exists.

Negotiating Favorable Payment Terms

Ensure proper payment cycle time period (e.g. 45 days).
Ensure invoices become due only upon properly submitted.
Ensure proper Company form of requisition of payment is used.
Ensure prompt payment discount provisions are available to Company.

Negotiating Favorable Retainage Terms

Ensure retainage (typically ten (10) percent).
Ensure retainage not payable until all Work fully completed.

Negotiating Favorable Offset / Setoff Terms

Ensure the right to offset / setoff against other Contracts.
Ensure the right to deduct for claims / backcharges / self-help / audit cost.

Obtaining Letters of Credit

Ensure letters of credit are from qualified institution.
Ensure letters of credit are in the form supplied by counsel.

Ensure letters of credit remain in effect through full warranty period.
Ensure original copy of letter of credit is appropriately filed.
Track expiration dates and ensure renewals are up to date.

Obtaining Parental Guaranty

Ensure parent guaranty are from qualified institution.
Ensure parent guaranty are in the form supplied by counsel.
Ensure parent guaranty remain in effect through full warranty period.
Ensure original copy of parental guaranty is appropriately filed.
Track expiration dates.

Obtaining Insurance Coverages

Obtain appropriate insurance coverages based upon risks involved.
Ensure certificates are on file, consistent with contractual requirements.
Track expiration dates and ensure renewals are up to date.

Payment and Performance Bonds

Payment and performance bonds should be used rarely and carefully. Such bonds are not "insurance" in the sense that the entity issuing the bond does not pay out claims based upon actuarial assumptions.

When bonds are used: (1) separate payment and performance bonds should be purchased, and (2) the form of payment and performance bonds should be obtained from or reviewed by counsel. Remember a bond is simply a form of contract and is negotiable.

Note that a bond is the surety's promise to the "obligee" (typically an owner) that the surety's "principal" (typically a contractor) will perform the contract. A bond (e.g., a payment and performance bond) is a contract between three entities: the owner, contractor, and surety, and each have respective rights and obligations. There is a whole body of law (the law of suretyship) applicable to this type of transaction. Obviously how the bond is worded makes a big difference in terms of what your rights and obligations are under a bond. All bonds are not "equal." Only use bonds that have been developed or approved by your counsel.

Remember that bonds can be expensive and that there may be other ways (like getting a guarantee from a "parent" with deep pockets that its subsidiary will perform) to manage the risks you are trying to protect yourself against. Also bear in mind that sureties don't expect to have to pay on a claim. Be aware that sureties can also assert any of the contractors' rights or claims and some have a history of being litigious, i.e., filing suits against project owners. Exercise caution, consult with counsel, and use a form of bond that suits your needs.

Key Risks to Consider

1. The failure to prioritize risks and integrate past learnings.

2. The failure to identify and access the risks to the supply chain.

3. The failure to integrate market intelligence with decision making.

Financial Risk Management Tools

1. Letters of Credit.

2. Parental Guarantees.

3. Payment and Performance Bonds.

Reporting Requirements

1. Require contractor risk contingency plans.

2. Require periodic risk self-assessment from contractors.

3. Require periodic meetings or teleconferences regarding risk.

4. Ensure that the preparation and submittal of contingency plans and self-assessment exercises as well as periodic reporting are specified and specific deliverables required under the contract.

CONTRACT DRAFTING GUIDELINES

All contracts have the same basic set of clauses regardless of what is being purchased or sold. These include warranty, indemnity, change, delays, termination, choice of law, venue, and other such typical provisions.

Each organization has its typical approach to these clauses ("boiler plate") which can be tailored to the particular circumstances of the individual transactions. However, certain clauses need to be individually developed for each contract.

Clauses That Need To Be Individually Developed For Each Commercial Transaction

1. Identification of the parties.
   What legal entities will be accountable?

2. Specifying what will be purchased or sold.
   What is the scope for work or deliverables to be provided?

3. Particular price and payment terms.
   Are prices for both present and future purchases covered?

4. Start, duration, and renewal terms.
   What are the start, end, and renewal dates?

5. Delivery, risk of loss, and shipment terms.
   When, where, and how will the deliverables be provided?

6. Performance or technical criteria and standards.
   What are the particular performance or technical requirements?

7. Inspection, test, or acceptance criteria and standards.
   How and when will conformity be established?

8. Special Commercial Terms Or Conditions.
   Are options, right of first refusal, liquidated damages, etc. . . needed?

9. Specifying the amount or quantity to be purchased.
   Quantity and how is it expressed? (amount, requirements, output)

10. Incorporation of representations.
    Are all important representations or documents included?

11. Future needs or requirements.
    Are changes in operations or technology adequately addressed?

12. Maintenance and replacement.
    What are the maintenance and inventory needs?

13. Reimbursable expenses.
    What is reimbursable and on what basis?

14. Unique risks.
    What could affect performance?

15. Authorized signature.
    Are the signatories duly authorized?

THE SCOPE OF WORK - DEFINING THE DELIVERABLES

A Good Beginning Makes for a Good Ending

"Scope is King" as the saying goes. Nothing is more important in terms of ensuring a good start for a good finish. Whether you're starting from a good scope of work or using the request for proposal (RFP) process to collect information and develop your scope of work, the quality of the scope is the single most important thing that will determine the relative success or failure of the transaction.

Who is responsible for writing the scope? This can be a problem for the SCM professional who is charged with issuing a contract but understandably lacks the skill and expertise needed to prepare a technical document which may require engineering, computer or other very specialized knowledge and expertise. In such cases, the buying entity has two choices: (a) utilize in-house expertise from the internal "client group" or, (b) hire a third-party to independently develop the scope (Note: No entity who is bidding on the work should be charged with developing the scope that others will be bidding on).

Either way the SCM professional will need to manage the situation and exercise appropriate control over the scope writing process. How can this be done? First and foremost the organization needs to be educated about just how critical the scope is to the entire process. It's the keystone to success. Secondly, the SCM professional can provide the person or entity authoring the scope with appropriate fill in the blank templates giving the author a written step by step process. Of course, even relatively "simple" equipment procurements can be technically complex especially to the uninitiated. The need for a template is also paramount in cases involving complex construction or service type transactions. The solution is to have at least two forms of templates; one for relatively simple transactions and another for more complex initiatives. Of course, no template is perfect and each may have to be slightly modified to fit the particular needs of the situation.

Everyone in the organization needs to understand what makes a "good" scope and why good scopes of work are important to ensure a successful transaction.

How To Evaluate A Scope Of Work

A well-defined Scope of Work ("SOW") which clearly spells out what is to be accomplished or delivered in terms of performance is crucial to any good contract management process. As such, the SOW should be evaluated as follows:

- Is the SOW clear?

- Is the SOW correct?

- Is the SOW complete?

- Is the SOW consistent?

- Is the SOW comprehensible?

Why The Scope Of Work Is So Important

Taking the time and effort to develop a well-articulated SOW is important because a SOW will:

- Be a part of the contract

- Be relied upon in competitive bidding

- Be used to allocate funds and set budgets

- Be used to judge whether performance is adequate

- Help avoid and minimize costly changes, delays, and disputes

SIMPLE STEPS FOR IMPROVING SCOPE OF WORK DOCUMENTS

Have a disciplined and defined process for developing your scope of work which might look like this:

1. Define what is to be performed.

2. Learn from and do not repeat past mistakes.

3. Link payments to performance or progress.

4. Develop a well-organized table of contents.

5. Clearly specify the objectives to be achieved.

6. Anticipate changes in needs or circumstances.

7. Seek input from the right people at the right time.

8. Specify the project plan, schedule and milestones.

9. Specify where the deliverables will be performed.

10. Avoid making any unintended (implied) warranties.

11. Specify the standards or performance requirements.

12. Specify the applicable testing or acceptance criteria.

13. Avoid incorrect, inconsistent, or contradictory statements.

14. Develop an order of precedence for the contract documents.

15. Anticipate the need for interpretation and who's judgment will govern.

WAYS TO IMPROVE SOW WORDING

Wording is obviously important in how a scope is written and simple changes can make big differences in terms of clarity and consistency. You should:

1. Avoid vague or inexact words or phrases.

2. Avoid inexact terms like "etc.." or "and/or".

3. Avoid using colloquialisms, "buzz words", or jargon.

4. Use the word "shall" to express the supplier's actions.

5. Use the word "will" to express the purchaser's actions.

6. Avoid using the words "should" or "may" to express actions.

7. Use words correctly (e.g., "mortar" vs. "grout").

8. Use words consistently (e.g., "brace" vs. "support").

9. Avoid using terms that do not have well-understood meanings.

10. Where possible, use a single word instead of several words.

Examples:

"To" vs. "In order to . . ."

"If" vs. "In the event that . . ."

"For" vs. "In the amount of . . ."

"Whether" vs. "Whether or not . . ."

SCOPE OF WORK CONSIDERATIONS

Every organization will have its own key scope of work considerations which might include as a minimum the following:

1. Define The Scope of Work To Be Performed.

Make sure the scope of work clearly and completely sets forth what is to be done. The scope or statement of work should specify all the duties and responsibilities including all work necessary to accomplish the project. If there are a lot of "change orders", it suggests the possibility of poor scope of work documents or lack of aggressive contract administration and contract measures.

2. Specify The Deliverables To Be Provided.

Specify the deliverables to be provided, including such details as the number, due date, and the like. One can specify that the deliverables will be in accordance with a particular model, sample, layout, or format.

3. Specify Where The Services/Goods Will Be Provided/Delivered.

It is useful to specify the location where the services will be performed in terms of a particular location or locations. Where the services will be provided may have an impact of both the direct and indirect cost of the services. Address where the goods are to be delivered and who has the risk of loss in transit. Don't rely on "FOB" abbreviations. Spell out who exactly is on the risk of loss in transit.

4. Set The Standards Governing Performance.

Set performance standards for goods or requirements and make sure they will meet operating requirements. Note that professionals (e.g., engineers) are usually expected to perform their services with the care, skill, and diligence in accordance with the applicable and currently recognized professional standards. That standard may or may not fit every need and is expressed in highly generalized terms. If a higher or more objective standard is required, it should be articulated.

5. Specify The Objectives To Be Achieved.

Obtain a guarantee of specific results. Remember that those engaged in professions are held only to the standards generally followed in their particular profession and are required only to exercise due care. They may, of course, be held for malpractice or negligent performance. However, the parties can agree to specific guarantees or that a particular result will be accomplished. Basically, pay for performance.

6. Be Careful What You Ask For.

You can contract for resources or results. Generally it is much better to define the contractor's responsibilities as producing a specific result as oppose to a level of effort. Also be careful when specifying a "standard" as opposed to "performance". The standard you specify may not be exactly what is needed and if too strict may end up costing you more than you need to pay. Remember to continuously test your assumptions.

7. Tailor The Contract To The Transaction.

Take time to carefully tailor the contract to the particular effort. Tailoring the contract means more than simply using a "cut and paste" approach. It means a clear and complete articulation of each party's rights and responsibilities. Contract documents which are incomplete, inconsistent, or inapplicable to the task can create problems. Also, be wary of standard form contracts prepared by trade associations representing architects, contractors, or engineers. These contracts usually do a good job of contractually protecting their respective "client" groups, but they may not meet your needs. Generally, you are much better off "controlling the paper" and developing your own contract rather than using someone else's document.

8. Identify The Success Factors.

A key step in planning a large-scale project or complex undertaking of any sort is to identify and prioritize the critical factors by which the success or failure of the project will be judged. The "mission" or objectives sought to be achieved should be clearly articulated, both internally and to the contractor with predetermined standards of performance. Note that the "success factors" and their relative importance may differ, depending on one's perspective.

9. Front-Load The Effort.

The old saying that "prevention is the best cure" is true in medicine and contracts. Spend enough time and effort on preparing a clear and complete document with a carefully written scope of work. The "cut and paste" method of preparing contracts can be dangerous. Avoid using outdated or inapplicable documents. It might be better to go to the expense of creating a well-crafted contract and avoid the cost of a failed project and subsequent "root cause" post mortem analysis. Poor scope documents can also drive costly changes and delays.

10. Know The Rules of Contract Interpretation.

Business people are constantly called upon to interpret contract clauses. The usual rules of contract interpretation are simple and reflect a common sense approach. The general basic rules are as follows:

The plain meaning governs.

The contract is construed as a whole.

The specific governs over the general.

Writings govern over figures or plans.

Exculpatory clauses are strictly construed.

The objective intent of the parties governs.

"Extrinsic" evidence (letters, memos, minutes, conduct, past practice, etc. . . .) can be used to interpret, but not to change or contradict the contract.

What is handwritten governs over what is typed and what is typed governs over preprinted text.

Course of performance (how you have acted under the deal in question) governs over course of dealing (how you have acted in past deals) which, in turn, governs over trade practice (how others in the business act). The beauty of a contract is that clearly expressed contract terms trump all!

How ambiguities are construed may also depend on who drafted the agreement, as well as whether ambiguities were obvious, or should have been, to the reader. A Contractor usually has a duty to inquire about any ambiguities in the contract documents, particularly where the ambiguity is obvious. Contracts can also reduce ambiguity by including an "order-of-precedence" clause identifying which documents govern in terms of priority.

11. Use Your Collective Corporate Experience.

Past experience, both in terms of what has worked or not worked well in other contracts, can help repeat earlier success and avoid past failures. Make sure that you use the entire "corporate" collective experience by keeping a list of "lessons learned" on past projects. Communicate. E-mail makes it easy to put everyone on "notice".

12. Be Specific about Any Site Requirements or Restrictions.

If the Company needs to perform any site preparation work, make sure the seller agrees that the deliverables will be compatible with the prepared site in terms of power needs, clearances, access, or environmental (temperature, humidity) needs or considerations. If there are restrictions to site access, specify what they are to the extent they are known.

INCORPORATING DOCUMENTS BY REFERENCE

Incorporating documents by reference can be a useful technique in putting together the set of contract documents that make up the agreement between the parties. When using this technique, bear in mind the following considerations:

1. What documents, or portions thereof, should be incorporated, and

2. What is the order of precedence in the event the documents contain inconsistencies?

Typical "incorporation by reference" contract language might read:

> "The contract between the Parties consists of this Agreement for XYZ which hereby incorporates by reference the following documents. The documents are to be construed as complimentary. However, in the event of any inconsistencies between the documents, they shall govern in the following order of precedence: This Agreement for XYZ and [LIST DOCUMENTS INCORPORATED BY REFERENCE IN ORDER OF PRECEDENCE.]"

The order of precedence for documents incorporated by reference should always be specified, particularly where the contract documents are lengthy or complex. This assists the parties (and if need be, the courts) to resolve any inconsistencies. Of course, the order of precedence is only relied upon if, in fact, there is an "inconsistency".

Provisions in a contract are "inconsistent" if they are "mutually repugnant", meaning that they contradict one to the other, so that both cannot apply and still have the agreement make sense. Contract provisions should not be construed as inconsistent unless no other reasonable interpretation is possible.

Given that both parties will be relying on the contract documents and their order of precedence, special care needs to be taken to ensure that the agreement correctly reflects the intent of the parties.

RULES FOR GOOD INCORPORATION BY REFERENCE

While incorporating documents by reference can be a useful technique in putting together a set of contract documents, it can also be a trap if not done correctly. The following rules of good incorporation by reference can help avoid unintended consequences and manage the expectations of the parties.

1. Ensure the documents are clearly identified by title and date.

2. Ensure the documents do not duplicate or reword information.

3. Ensure the documents being incorporated are clear and complete.

4. Ensure all the documents have been read together as an integrated whole.

5. Ensure the documents being incorporated do not contradict one another.

6. Ensure the documents are correctly referenced throughout the contract.

7. Ensure all the documents are listed in one place in their order of precedence.

8. Ensure that all the documents are readily accessible by those who will be relying on them to manage the contract.

9. Avoid wholesale incorporation of supplier's proposals without deleting objectionable conditions, assumptions, limitations, exceptions, or inconsistencies.

10. Avoid incorporating documents that have yet to be created, which are subject to some future "mutual agreement" between the parties, or which can be unilaterally changed by a party or by third parties.

REVIEW OF KEY CONSIDERATIONS WHEN WRITING A SOW

1. **Remember what a scope of work is.** The scope of work is that part of a contract that defines what the person or entity (e.g. consultant, contractor, supplier) performing the work is to provide, perform or otherwise accomplish. For ease of reference we will use the term "Contractor" in this text. Workscopes are typically found in construction contracts but have application in other transactions such as consulting agreements, service agreements or equipment purchases.

2. **Results versus resources.** Workscopes come in two basic types; for results or resources. A results-oriented workscope focuses on and defines success by a specific "result" in terms of what the Contractor is to achieve as an outcome. A resource-oriented workscope promises a level of effort or "resources", but not a specific result. For example, typically an EPC contract promises a result for a firm fixed price. By contrast, a consulting services agreement promises advice or work on an hourly or task basis but usually does not guarantee an outcome.

3. **Specification versus performance.** A workscope can contain "specification" standards, "performance" standards or a mixture of both. For example, the workscope could require that the Contractor comply with certain published industry codes or requirements or follow

certain processes or procedures. The workscope could also require that the product/system/facility meet specific performance or acceptance criteria or tests. Be careful when setting standards. Setting the wrong standard, or setting standards that are too low or too high, can have adverse consequences.

4. **Why is the scope of work so important?** Workscopes are a key part of the contract and form the basis for pricing the work to be performed. Workscopes are relied upon in competitive bidding and used to allocate funds, set budgets and measure performance. A good workscope also helps avoid, minimize and manage claims, changes and delays. For example, the first step in determining whether a claim for "extra" work is truly in addition to what was required would be to review the workscope. Bear in mind that one day the workscope may be placed in front of a judge and jury.

5. **Clarity and consistency.** The essential purpose of a contract is to set forth the respective responsibilities of the parties with precision for a predictable outcome. Accordingly, Workscopes need to be clear so that subsequent readers who were not involved in its preparation will have the same understanding as the author(s).

6. **Avoid ambiguity.** Use simple well-understood terms and words consistently and avoid colloquialisms or "buzz words". Saying it once correctly avoids ambiguity and needless repetition. (e.g. "brace" vs. "support"; "mortar" vs. "grout"). Avoid using in-exact terms like "etc.", "and/or", "best efforts", "reasonable", "unrestricted", "adequate" or the like. Use "shall" to express what the Contractor is obligated to do and, if applicable, "will" to indicate what the owner is to provide. Don't use "should" or "may" to express required actions. Don't use abbreviations unless they are defined in the contract.

7. **Pay attention to definitions.** How terms like "Work", "Materials", "Warranty" and the like are defined is crucial to a good workscope. Remember that the workscope is a part of the contract and that there may be definitions in other parts of the contract, particularly in the commercial terms and conditions. Make sure you don't trip over these definitions and that the key words are defined the same way in all sections of the contract. Avoid referring to the same thing using different terms (e.g. "ABC Corp." or "Contractor").

8. **Watch out for multiple authors.** Often different sections of the workscope are written by different persons. Everyone has their own writing style and sometimes these multiple authors don't read what the others have written. The net result is a workscope that is far from seamless and which lacks the essential clarity and consistency we strive for. Have one person be in charge of proofreading and integrating the entire document by giving it a "cold" read.

9. **Test your assumptions.** The biggest mistake is to assume that the current project or procurement you are working on is going to be "just the same" as the last one. The temptation is not to test that assumption and to either copy or "cut and paste" from the last project's workscope. Better to apply good "lessons learned" rather than simply copy what was done before. The key is to tailor the workscope to the particular circumstances of the situation and job.

10. **Use a table of contents, numbering system and logical document hierarchy.** Every good workscope has a table of contents and each paragraph is numbered. This helps in the administration and management of the contract down the road. Avoid using bullets or un-numbered forms of identifying paragraphs or sections of the workscope. Obviously, each page should be numbered. Identify

which documents will govern in the unlikely event of a conflict or inconsistency.

11. **Be Brief.** The words "the" and "that" are two of the most overused words in the English language and are not always necessary. Examples of other ways to shorten contract documents include using: "To" vs "In order to..."; "If" vs "In the event that..."; "For" vs "In the amount of..."; "Whether" vs "Whether or not..."; "Any" vs "Any and all...". Nor is it necessary to continually repeat the phrase "It is understood and agreed that...". Definitions can also help achieve brevity. Terms like "Including" can be defined as "Including but not limited to..." and "Notice" can be defined to mean written notice to avoid needless repetition.

12. **Be Consistent.** As noted above, proper use of definitions can promote consistency. Often contract documents require the work meet with the company's "approval" or "satisfaction" followed by words like "in the company's sole judgment and discretion". Be consistent and if you mean "in the company's sole judgment and discretion" either define "approval" or "satisfaction" to include that requirement or repeat the phrase every time.

13. **Be Clear.** Contracts often include cross references to other documents or sections of the contract. Have a consistent protocol for how you refer to those other documents or sections. If your contract contains exhibits that relate to a specific paragraph in the contract (e.g. "Article 23, par 1"), you can identify and tie that exhibit to the specific paragraph, e.g. "Exhibit 23.1". Avoid identifying different documents the same way (e.g. "Exhibit 1", "Attachment 1", "Appendix 1"). There should only be one "Exhibit 1", "Attachment 1", "Appendix 1".

14. Be Careful About What is Incorporated by Reference. Not every document referenced in the workscope necessarily becomes part of the contract. Some documents such as reports or information obtained from third parties may be provided for "informational purposes only".

15. Specify Any Training Requirements. If appropriate, specify the number of persons to be trained, when and where the training will take place, its duration and whether it will be continuous or segmented, the nature and number of the training materials and manuals, the qualifications of those doing the training and how travel or other expenses will be handled.

16. Read and Understand the "Entire Agreement" Clause. That clause states that the whole deal is reflected in the contract. Make sure that is true. Often things are said or presentations made that contain representations that are important to the project or procurement. Make sure all of those important representations make it into the final contract to avoid the "But you said…" trap.

17. Avoid Unwise Commitments. Be careful and specific when promising to provide equipment, facilities, manpower or other resources to assist the contractor. Generally, it is safest to limit the company's obligation to paying for work conforming to the contract. If you do make commitments, make sure they are specific and limited. For example, it is better to provide a defined lay-down area in the form of a map than to promise "adequate" lay-down area. If the company does have responsibilities under the contract, specify that unless otherwise specifically stated, any task or activity necessary to perform the work is the contractor's responsibility. In effect make it clear that any action or activity not specifically identified as the company's responsibility is the Contractor's.

18. Should you Include Proposals as Part of the Workscope? The short answer is "no". The longer is "rarely and carefully". Watch out for imbedded "assumptions" or "clarifications". In addition, proposals often become outdated. At a minimum, review the proposal for outdated or incorrect information, or content which is inconsistent with the company's objectives. As a safeguard, specify the order of precedence, e.g. "In the event of a conflict between the contract documents, the company's commercial terms and conditions shall govern".

19. When Does an Equipment Purchase Require a Workscope? Sometimes more than just delivering equipment is involved. There may be installation work, testing protocols, acceptance criteria and training requirements justifying putting in the time and effort to develop a good workscope.

20. Consider an Introductory Statement. Obviously the introductory statement would depend in part on the type of contract, such as Engineer Procure and Construct (EPC), Guaranteed Maximum Price (GMP), Time and Materials (T&M) or the like. As a starting point it might read something like this:

Workscope

1. The scope of work to be provided under this Contract consists of the Work specified in the Contract, including Exhibit A, and all other work, activities, items or materials which may be required to successfully complete the Work specified and all other requirements of the Contract. The objective of this Contract is to relieve the Company of the necessity of engaging in any activities or work or supplying any labor, services or material to complete the Work; unless expressly stated herein as being furnished by the Company.

2. It is the intent of the parties that the Contractor [engineer, design, procure, project manage, construct, test, start-up and commission a highly reliable (facility) in accordance with this Contract.] The Contractor shall perform all of the Work specified or implied by this Contract in order to accomplish the intent of the parties. The Contractor's performance under this Contract shall include everything requisite and necessary to complete the entire Work notwithstanding the fact that every item involved may not be specifically mentioned. Details and items not indicated herein shall be adequately and properly performed by the Contractor at no extra cost if such details or items are necessary to complete the Work.

21. **Conclusion.** Scope is king. By putting in the "up-front" effort to prepare a workscope that is clear, concise and complete you will save time and treasure in the long run. The worst mistake you can make is to assume that the company's needs and expectations are "understood". Time and experience have demonstrated that undocumented or vague "understandings" lead to misunderstandings and disputes. Memories fade and people change. The individuals who negotiated the contract may not be the same ones who are living with and administering the contract. Remember too that the contract, including the workscope, may one day be read and interpreted by others in the context of a claim or lawsuit.

KEY QUESTIONS TO ASK WHEN DEVELOPING SCOPE

Whether or not you are technical or subject matter expert, you can always define the scope in terms of the outcome you want to achieve. By asking yourself, or other technically minded team members, the following questions you can increase the quality of your scope of work documents. Obviously the list will vary slightly depending upon what is being purchased, built or installed and not all questions have applicability to all potential transactions.

1. What are the RESULTS to be achieved?
2. What are the respective RESPONSIBILITIES?
3. What are the start, end, delivery and milestone DATES?
4. How is PAYMENT tied to PERFORMANCE?
5. What are the SITE, ACCESS, or ENVIRONMENTAL conditions?
6. Where will DELIVERY or PERFORMANCE be made?

7. What are the REPORTING requirements?
8. What are the TEST and ACCEPTANCE criteria?
9. What are the INFORMATION requirements?
10. What are the TRAINING requirements?
11. What are the TRANSPORTATION requirements?

12. What are the STORAGE requirements?
13. Who are the KEY PERSONNEL?
14. What are the required ACCURACY levels?
15. How RUGGED does the equipment need to be?
16. What is the WORK PLAN for getting it done?

17. What are the MAINTENANCE requirements?
18. What are the SPARE PART requirements?
19. Are there special INSTALLATION requirements?
20. What are the RELIABILITY requirements?
21. What are the UTILITY requirements?
22. What are the COMPATIBILITY requirements?
23. What are the SERVICE LEVEL requirements?
24. Where are the user or operating MANUALS?
25. Where is the SOURCE CODE?
26. [OTHER]?

KEY COMPENSATION CONCEPTS

There are several key compensation concepts that need to be addressed in practically every transaction. Thus, most if not all contracts should recite that:

1. Contract Price. Contractor shall not be entitled to any payment, reimbursement, or other compensation except as specified in this Contract. Contractor's compensation shall not exceed the dollar amount of the Contract Price of [__] plus any additional Work authorized by written Change Order.

2. Rental Costs. For Work done on a time and materials basis or Work done on a cost plus basis, Company will reimburse Contractor for the cost of Contractor-rented equipment, used for the Work, plus a [__] percent ([__]%) fee on the actual cost of rental.

3. Material Costs. For Work done on a time and materials basis or Work done on a cost plus basis, Company will reimburse Contractor for the actual cost of: (a) Contractor-purchased Material plus a [__] percent ([__]%) fee and (b) Subcontractors plus a [__] percent ([__]%) fee. Contractor shall not purchase Material or perform Work with Subcontractors without the Company's prior written consent.

4. Open-Book Review. For lump sum extra work or Work done on a time and materials basis or Work done on a cost plus basis, Contractor shall provide its pricing estimate for the extra work or Work on a full open-book basis, including all Contractor labor, equipment and material breakdown which shall include all overheads, profits, taxes, fees, insurances, productivity levels and any other related cost information, for the Company's review. For Work done on a time materials basis or Work done on a cost plus basis, Company shall be entitled to receive Contractor's certified payroll, in an electronic native file format capable of manipulation, confirming the amounts paid to workers or Contractor's employees.

5. Insurance Costs. Insurance costs for Work done on a time and materials basis or Work done on a cost plus basis Contractor's general liability insurance cost shall be calculated as a percentage of the Contractor's gross receipts allocated to the Work to be performed under the Contract. The Contractor shall attach no profit or markup to the cost of this or any other insurance costs or premiums and shall ensure that Company only pays its allocable share. The Company shall under no circumstances be billed more than [___] percent ([___]%) of Contractor's gross receipts to cover its general liability insurance costs.

6. Worker's Compensation. Contractor's Worker's Compensation Insurance Costs shall be calculated as a percentage of the Contractor's gross payroll costs allocated to the Work to be performed under the Contract.

7. Wages and Taxes. The Contract Price shall include any [State] sales and use tax. In no event shall Company be responsible for or reimburse Contractor or any of its Subcontractors for any corporate franchise, net income, import duty, or similar taxes imposed upon Contractor, including Subcontractors, for the general privilege of conducting business. Under no circumstances will the Company be liable for charges for any: (a) taxes

never actually paid to the applicable taxing authority; (b) wages paid to craft workers in excess of the applicable craft rate for their classification, (c) taxes billed in excess of wage rate limits, or (d) charges for wages not actually paid, or (e) charges for cost or expenses not actually incurred.

8. Company Work. Any Work, including Materials, provided by Company due to Contractor's failure to perform shall be charged to Contractor at the Company's cost, plus a fee of [____] ([__]) percent.

9. Miscellaneous. Except in the case of firm fixed price, lump sum Work, Contractor agrees to: (a) collect all allowable refunds, rebates, and discounts on Materials, containers, and other items received in connection with the Work, and (b) pay all invoices in time to take advantage of all cash discounts and credit any amounts owed by the Company to Contractor by all such refunds, rebates, and discounts. All applications for payment should certify that all such refunds, rebates, and discounts have been credited to the Company, said credit being shown as a separate line item. If Contractor fails or neglects to take any discount or collect any refund or rebate offered, the sum so lost shall be credited to the Company.

10. Change Management. The single best way to control costs after a contract is signed is to ensure that the proper change management provisions have been built into the agreement. This would include the right to increase or decrease the scope of work and associated schedule at some agreed upon price for both additional work and reductions in work or changes in schedule. Consider requiring Contractors to obtain competitive market pricing for changes performed by Subcontractors. For cost plus work, Contractors, at request of the Company, should provide all Subcontractor bids to the Company on an "open book" basis. For changes performed by Subcontractors, Subcontractors' mark-up for overhead and profit should not exceed that of the Contractor. No mark-up for overhead and profit should be

applied to the premium of Subcontractor's overtime costs. There should be no mark-up applied to taxes or other expenses that are simply reimbursable.

11. Restocking Fee. Any restocking fee charged by Contractor shall not exceed the lesser of: (a) five percent (5%) of the Purchase Price attributable to the Equipment or materials suspended or (b) one percent (1%) of the total Purchase Price.

12. Time of performance is of the essence. If, at any time, Contract Administrator and the Company determine that the Work is behind schedule, the Contractor shall increase its forces, work overtime, add shifts, or otherwise take all necessary steps to get the Work back on schedule at no additional cost to the Company.

The list noted above is not exhaustive and obviously additional items can be added or the wording of the recommended additions amended to ensure applicability.

Negotiating Price

All aspects of a transaction, including contract type, risk allocation, scope of respective responsibilities and obligations as well as schedule or time frame for performance affect price. It is often difficult to determine what is a "good" price. Price can best be ascertained and tested by competition and / or open-book access to relevant and timely data.

Remember that negotiating price may not be a one-time effort. Once the deal is done and terms have been agreed to, negotiating future price changes can be a challenge. Negotiate price when leverage is at its highest which may be at the very beginning of the contract lifecycle. For example, the best time to negotiate option pricing for future spare or replacement parts or future services may be when the original contract is negotiated.

Note that price escalation based on indices such as the CPI may have no bearing on the provider's actual cost given the make-up of the index. Negotiate price adjustments that can go up or down based on an accurate index that correctly reflects the actual cost increase or decrease.

Understand the Cost Drivers

It is important to understand what may be driving costs for either or both internal and external factors. These may include supply and demand, as well as completion and bidding. A key question to address is whether there are requirements imposed on suppliers that drive costs but add little value (e.g. excessive recordkeeping requirements, gold-plating, silly or poorly written specifications, etc.). In order to make the best use of time and effort one approach is to perform a price analysis for lower dollar-value items and a cost analysis for higher-dollar items. A key success factor in negotiating price is to find reliable sources of pricing data, understand the competitive landscape as well as sound preparation. It's also important to be creative and to explore innovative solutions and opportunities. These may include bartering or buyback arrangements as well as negotiating multi-year contracts with option pricing for future purchases. Bear in mind that material costs may be a relatively small component of total cost. There may also be hidden margins in overhead charges.

Baseline the Effort

Don't be afraid of the word "No". "No" is the word that sets the baseline for progress either as a floor or ceiling. There is nothing mean about saying no. By saying no you will get to the end game more quickly even if saying or hearing no can be stressful. Recognize that price negotiation can be a stressful discussion and focus on understanding the other side and why they believe what they do. Don't assume that the other side is malicious. The parties should explore ways to create new opportunities, reduce or defer costs or risks, increase benefits to other side, accelerate benefits to other side, increase the perception of the likelihood of benefits, remind the other party that there could be negative consequences for failure to resolve and reduce benefits if there is no agreement. Likewise, the effect of leverage cannot be overemphasized.

Finally, avoid the typical influencing traps including selling your position without understanding theirs, trying too hard to get to "yes" before understanding "no", spending time trying to influence people who can't be influenced (by you) and wasting time trying to influence people who can't decide what to do. Price negotiation more than any other type of negotiation depends on good information or preparation.

Transactions based upon Reimbursement

In cases where the Contractor is going to be compensated based upon reimbursement for its costs together with a fee to cover profit and overhead a key consideration is what costs are going to be reimbursed and which of those costs are going to be reimbursed with fee. Here are the three (3) basic scenarios:

Contractor's Costs to be Reimbursed with Fee. Typically, the Company reimburses the contractor for certain enumerated costs. Accordingly, these costs would include those listed below which are approved in advance by the company and paid directly by the contractor necessarily incurred in the prosecution of the work. The fee, as provided for in the contract, usually only applies to the following costs:

1. Base Labor Rate, excluding any benefits, fringes and taxes paid at straight time rates to labor employed directly by the Contractor in the performance of the Work;

2. Salaries, at rates previously approved by the Company, of Contractor's employees stationed at the site of the Work, in whatever capacity employed;

3. Remuneration, at rates previously approved by the Company, for the time actually spent at the project site by Contractor, or a member of the firm or officer of Contractor, in the capacity of job supervisor when requested by the Company;

4. The previously approved cost to Contractor of Materials which become part of the Work provided under the Contract except those cost which are included as part of equipment rental rates;

5. The cost to the Contractor of all subcontracts, but not fees paid to Subcontractors doing Work on a reimbursable T&M or cost plus basis. (See Section below entitled "Contractor's Costs to be Reimbursed Without Fee");

6. The rental cost of vehicles, trucks, or equipment not owned by Contractor or any of its affiliates, incurred in the performance of the Work at rates approved by the Company as set forth below:

    a. Rental rates for vehicles, trucks or equipment in all cases includes necessary fuel, maintenance, lubricants, and other consumables, as approved by the Company prior to use thereof. The base labor rate of drivers are to be itemized separately and not be included in the rental rate. Where an operator trained in the use of a unit of construction equipment is required, his or her base labor rate may be included on the rental rate (e.g. crane operator), if requested and approved by the Company.

b. Where overtime use is made of a vehicle, truck, or other piece of equipment which includes the straight time pay of its driver or operator in its rental rate, the pay of the driver or operator for the overtime period above their straight time are to be shown separately on any bill.

7. For Contractor owned vehicle, trucks or equipment, the rate charged to Company includes Contractor's fee. The Company's total liability for Contractor owned or rented vehicles, trucks or equipment, under no circumstances, exceeds the fair market value of any vehicles, trucks, equipment, or any other items rented, whether such rented items are provided by Contractor directly or through some third party.

8. Rental rates are based on [XXX] hours per month. Company is only to be billed on an hour by hour basis for the time equipment was actually used in the performance of the Work, or in the case of stand-by time at rates specified in the Contract.

9. Rental rates include any and all component, consumables, accessory, constituent, adjunct and subordinate parts of equipment or machinery which may be necessary or required to perform the Work.

10. Expense of loading, unloading, erecting, dismantling, and hauling the Contractor's equipment and tools from the Contractor's office, storeroom, or yard to the site of the Work and return;

11. The cost of equipment or tools purchased or rented by the Contractor, with the approval in advance of purchase or rental by the Company, to be used exclusively on the Work, less salvage or resale value approved by the Company;

12. The rental of construction trailers and portable sanitary facilities approved in advance of rental by the Company.

Contractor's Costs to be Reimbursed without Fee. The Company reimburses the Contractor, without fee, for all costs described below which are approved by the Company as necessarily incurred for the proper prosecution of the Work and paid directly by the Contractor:

1. All applicable Federal, State and Local taxes or charges levied on Contractor and based on wages or salaries of labor employed for said Work which Contractor is required by law to pay; provided that (1) at any time during a tax year when the combined payments to any employee, whether on Work for Company or for others, equal the amount fixed by law on which such taxes are levied, Contractor makes no further charge to Company for this purpose on account of such employee, and (2) unemployment taxes are computed at the statutory rate or at the Contractor's merit rate, whichever is lower. Contractor must notify Company immediately of any change in its merit rate and the date it becomes effective;

2. Fees paid to Subcontractors doing Work on a reimbursable basis which fees must not exceed the percentage fee paid to the Contractor;

3. Permit fees, royalties, Worker's Compensation, Insurance premiums;

4. Sales, transportation, and all other direct taxes, including those paid by Subcontractors;

5. Premium rates and associated extra costs;

6. Payments for telegraph and telephone service, water, utilities, express, cartage, freight, and postage incurred in the performance of the Work.

Contractor's Costs not to be Reimbursed. Typically a Company does not reimburse the Contractor for, nor pay it a fee on, any of the following costs:

1. Salary of any employee or officer of Contractor, except as listed in the Section above entitled, "Contractor's Costs to be Reimbursed With Fee";

2. Salary and expenses of any person employed in Contractor's main office;

3. Overhead, or general costs or expenses of any kind, except those which may be properly included in, "Contractor's Costs to be Reimbursed With Fee" or, "Contractor's Costs to be Reimbursed Without Fee";

4. All taxes of any kind such as, but not limited to, income tax, franchise tax, or tax imposed for the general privilege of doing business;

5. Cost of repairs or replacement of construction equipment used on the Work, that is owned, rented, or leased by Contractor;

6. Losses and expense incurred through fault and neglect of Contractor, its employees, agents, and Subcontractors or any of them, including theft of tools or equipment, excessive labor cost, warranty work, and repair of damage to property of Company or of others occasioned by Contractor;

8. All costs or expenses incurred by Contractor or any Subcontractor due to infringement or violation of patents, copyrights, or other proprietary interests;

9. All costs or expenses incurred by Contractor or any Subcontractor in connection with any defense, indemnification, and hold harmless provisions of the Contract;

10. All other costs or expenses of any kind not specifically specified under the Contract as reimbursable, either with or without fee.

Costs paid directly by Company. Typically, the costs of the following items are paid for directly by the Company and no fee is paid to the Contractor for:

1. Material the Company may elect to purchase directly;

2. Contracts placed by the Company with others.

3. Equipment supplied by Company.

T & M Work: Key Considerations

As a general rule, Time and Materials (T & M) work presents more risk for buyer and requires more performance monitoring by buyer than firm, fixed price (lump sum) contracts. Key considerations include:

1. Are the rates competitive? (Bid?).

2. What will motivate efficiency, accuracy and completion? If you consider performance incentives, negotiate these at the end and make part

of the Contractor's T&M compensation at risk (in the areas of schedule adherence, productivity, safety, cost, etc.)

3. Ensure roles, responsibilities and scope are clear (i.e. how does the Contractor plan to staff the project and what are the respective functions; who is billable; who is not billable).

4. Devote adequate staff to monitor and control.

5. Hold regular status meetings to ensure issues are surfaced and accountability is understood.

6. Require estimated cost/duration of job prior to entering into contract. Use this information for performance metrics if incentives are used.

7. Consider GMP, targeted hours, volume discount.

8. Get built up rates (your form) and pay mark-up on base wage rate only.

9. Verify that work was actually performed and properly done.

10. Verify that the charges are correctly calculated in accordance with contract price, terms, rates, discounts, and other terms. Where contractor may be working on multiple jobs with differing compensation provisions, ensure no hidden double billing is occurring.

11. Require reasonable documentation to support that the work was done.

12. Sign off on work/time sheets DAILY.

13. Require notice of "non-standard" or "out-of-scope" work.

14. Watch out for incorrect "sales tax" charges on "capital improvements".

15. Watch out for redundant/duplicate billing.

16. Consider a certification:

    "I hereby certify that the billing statement is accurate, that the work has been fully and properly performed, in strict compliance with the contract standards and requirements, and that the amount billed is accurate, not duplicative and consistent with the contract terms, including all discounts or credits owed."

17. Ensure you have the right to terminate for convenience and take possession of any work products completed as of date of termination.

18. Put firm ends on amount permitted to be expended and dates through which agreement applies.

19. Watch out for common mistakes such as:

    (a) applying incorrect rate (e.g. foreman vs. journeyman)
    (b) applying incorrect overhead/profit markup rates
    (c) splitting and compounding overhead or other charges
    (d) applying incorrect federal and state payroll taxes
    (e) continuing to bill for certain payroll taxes beyond statutory limits
    (f) failing to confirm actual base rate by reviewing union wage bulletins
    (g) including workers compensation/liability insurance charges hourly in both rates and as a separate line item

(h) applying overhead/profit fees to loaded instead of base labor rates

(i) inappropriately charging sales tax on labor

(j) incorrectly billing a credit owed to the Company as a debit

(k) payment without adequate review or supporting documentation

20. Watch out for games being played with per diem (e.g. using relatives' or vacation homes as addresses) and expense accounts (e.g. incorporating vendor's expense reimbursement policy which is loose or contradicts yours).

CONTRACT ADMINISTRATION

A big part of contract management is administering the terms and conditions of the contract. Often, the real art of the deal is not doing the deal but instead living with the deal in the best possible way. A few simple steps can assist in that effort.

Prior To The Start Of Work

1. <u>Assemble</u> a copy of all the contract documents.

2. <u>Read</u> all the contract documents at least 3 times.

3. <u>Ensure</u> the scope of work is clear and complete.

4. <u>Ensure</u> the contractor has signed the agreement.

5. <u>Ensure</u> the correct insurance certificates are on file.

After The Start Of Work

6. <u>Respond</u> to all correspondence promptly.

7. <u>Ensure</u> contractor is promptly paid sums owed.

8. <u>Adhere</u> strictly to the change order requirements.

9. <u>Document</u> all important discussions and decisions.

10. <u>Provide</u> notice of any breach or deficient performance.

11. <u>Avoid</u> waiving or inadvertently relinquishing contract rights.

12. <u>Avoid</u> promising the contractor's subcontractors they will be paid.

13. <u>Avoid</u> directly controlling contractor's employees or sub-contractors.

14. <u>Avoid</u> apparent authority and manage the change order process.

CONTROLLING CHANGES

Maintaining control includes controlling the process of change. The following steps can be a useful part of controlling and minimizing changes.

Contract Rights

1. Start with a clear and complete scope of work.

2. Reserve the right to add to or delete from the work.

3. Set the price or credit due for extra or deleted work.

4. Require that changes be duly authorized in writing.

5. Require written notice of alleged or implied changes.

6. Specify that changes will not be a basis on which to claim delays.

7. Require that any claims be filed within a certain period of time.

8. Exclude liability for consequential damages such as loss of profits, productivity, and increased costs or overhead expenses.

9. Determine whether changes are really extra or out of scope work.

10. Specify that payment for any changes is full compensation for all charges arising from the change.

11. Avoid statements or conduct which could be construed as implied changes waiving the need for a writing.

12. Avoid making changes that are so substantial (cardinal) that they change the very essence of the contract into a different deal.

CHANGE MANAGEMENT

The process for dealing with changes and claims should be addressed in the commercial terms and conditions. When dealing with potential changes follow the process laid out in the contract and be mindful of the concepts and questions which follow. It is also important to seek appropriate guidance from the subject matter experts such as technical, insurance, risk management and legal and get management approval.

Changes and the consequences of changes can be minimized by the following:

1. Define the requirements for changes:

   a. Written notice
   b. Contract change request form
   c. Timely submittal of supporting documentation.

2. Define a "Change Order" as the Company's written authorization to the contractor signed by a duly authorized Company employee to make changes to the work or contract. Note the distinction between a contractor's "request for change" and

the company's change order granting, in whole or in part, that request.

3. Have a process for collecting and addressing requests for changes including acceptance or rejection where appropriate and keep careful records of same.

4. Consult with subject matter experts and keep management apprised.

5. Provide notice of deficient performance and request corrective action. Document all important discussions and decisions and follow up to ensure correction or application of other remedy.

6. Designate single point of contact (commercial/technical) for each party.

7. Ask the right questions regarding claims.

SAMPLE CHANGE MANAGEMENT PROCESS

1. Company shall have the right during the progress of the Work to order extra Work, including Materials, and to make alterations, additions, omissions, deletions, modifications, changes, or departures in the scope, schedule, sequence, method, or performance of the Work, including Materials, or make changes in any specifications, plans, or drawings, that it may desire, without invalidating the Contract, and Contractor agrees to effect all such changes. Any such changes the Company elects to make shall be by Change Order issued by the Company.

2. THE CONTRACTOR SHALL NOT PERFORM EXTRA WORK NOR SUPPLY EXTRA MATERIAL UNLESS A WRITTEN CHANGE ORDER THEREFORE SHALL HAVE BEEN OBTAINED PRIOR TO THE PERFORMANCE OF SUCH EXTRA WORK OR THE FURNISHING OF SUCH EXTRA MATERIAL. THE FAILURE TO COMPLY WITH THIS REQUIREMENT SHALL CONSTITUTE A WAIVER OF ANY CLAIM FOR ADDITIONAL COMPENSATION.

3. In the event Contractor believes it is entitled to a Change Order and prior to performing any out of scope work, Contractor shall submit to Company or Contract Administrator a Change Request in the form of Exhibit [__]. The failure to submit said Change Request prior to the performance of any out of scope work, shall operate as a waiver of Contractor's right to any additional compensation or time to perform.

4. The value of changes which decrease the scope of Work shall be determined by mutual agreement and deducted from the Contract Price. The value of changes or extras which increase the scope of Work shall be determined in accordance with subparagraph 6 below and shall be added to the Contract Price. In the event that changes do not involve extra costs, no additional compensation will be paid to the Contractor.

5. Changes which reduce the quantity of Work, including Materials, to be provided shall not constitute a claim for damages or for anticipated or lost profits on the Work involved in such reductions, and the Company shall be entitled to a credit on the Contract Price for the value of the omitted Work, including Materials, but subject to an allowance to the Contractor for any actual loss incurred by it in connection with the purchase, rental, delivery, and subsequent disposal of Materials planned, but which could not be used in any of the Work actually performed as a result of such changes.

6. Where changes or extras increase the quantity of Work, including Materials, to be provided beyond that required by the Contract, such increase shall be paid for by the Company, at the Company's option, by one of the following methods:

    a. Method A   By lump sum to be agreed to or,

    b. Method B   By agreeing to an amount applying; (i) unit price(s) or (ii) time and material rates, reflected herein, or

    c. Method C   If Method A or Method B cannot be agreed to, the Contractor shall be compensated at its direct cost plus five (5%) percent for overhead and profit.

7. The Company shall have the right to have the Contractor provide lump sum pricing for changes or extra work broken down in the format set forth in Exhibit [__].

8. The Company may direct the form in which accounts of costs shall be kept and may also specify the method of doing the extra Work and the type and kind of Materials, if required, which shall be used in the performance of the extra Work. The compensation paid to the Contractor under Methods A, B, or C shall be deemed to constitute full and complete compensation for the Contractor's profit, overhead, superintendence, general foremen, foremen, office expenses, and all other elements of costs or expenses for Work, including Materials.

9. For changes compensated on a time and material basis the following provisions apply:

a. Rental rates for third-party equipment used by Contractor for performance of changes shall be approved by Company prior to rental and will be reimbursed at actual cost to Contractor, including transportation to site, as substantiated by invoices certified paid or by such documentation as may be required by Company or Contract Administrator, plus a mark-up for all overhead and profit of Contractor thereon of five percent (5%). Prior to any third-party rental, Contractor shall submit a stated value for the equipment being rented and demonstrate the rates to be favorable on a competitive basis.

b. Subcontracts and third-party services employed by Contractor for performance of changes shall be approved by Company or Contract Administrator prior to use and will be reimbursed at actual cost to Contractor as substantiated by invoices certified paid or by such documentation as may be required by Company or Contract Administrator, plus a mark-up for all overhead and profit of Contractor thereon of five percent (5%).

c. Compensation for additional Materials shall be at actual invoiced cost to Contractor, including transportation to site, as substantiated by invoices certified paid or by such documentation as may be required by Company or Contract Administrator, plus a single mark-up of five percent (5%) for overhead and profit. Contractor shall provide proof of competitive pricing for all Materials furnished.

10. Contractor shall obtain competitive market pricing for changes performed by Subcontractors. Contractor, at request of the Company or Contract Administrator, shall provide all Subcontractor bids to the Company or Contract Administrator on an "open book" basis. For changes performed by Subcontractors, Subcontractors' mark-up

for overhead and profit shall not exceed that of the Contractor. No mark-up for overhead and profit shall be applied to the premium of Subcontractor's overtime costs. There shall be no mark-up applied to taxes.

11. If the Contractor claims that any order, act, or omission of the Company or Contract Administrator will increase expenses, costs or Work, including Materials, Contractor shall give Company and Contract Administrator Written Notice thereof within three (3) business days after such order, act, or omission. Not later than fifteen (15) calendar days after such Written Notice is received by Company and Contract Administrator, Contractor shall submit to Company and Contract Administrator, a detailed statement of the cost of the extra work claimed to be required, as well as any impact to the Work schedule, together with supporting documents and information which clearly and convincingly supports Contractor's claim. The failure to fully comply with the requirements for a Written Notice or the failure to provide a detailed statement as specified within the times set forth herein shall constitute a waiver of any claim for additional compensation. The Company's or Contract Administrator's knowledge of the condition or event giving rise to any claims of extra expense, cost or Work shall not affect the requirement for Written Notice. Company shall not be charged for the costs or expenses of providing Written Notice, requesting changes to this Contract, or making any claims arising out of this Contract.

FORCE MAJEURE

Many contracts provide that the parties are not be liable to each other for any breach or failure to perform the contract due to "Force Majeure". Basically, Force Majeure is an excuse which negates the obligation to perform. Obviously, the critical factor is how Force Majeure is defined. Buyers typically want a narrow definition while suppliers typically want a broad definition.

Force Majeure can be defined as any occurrence beyond the reasonable control of either party which prevents performance, including fire; flood; explosion; strike; labor dispute; war; sabotage; riot; damage to or failure of major equipment, plants, piping, or appurtenances; unavailability of transportation facilities; acts of God; delay or failure to act by governmental authority, including legislation, regulation, or final judgment of a court of law. This definition can be broadened by adding language such as: "whether or not the same or similar to the occurrences listed herein".

The contract should recite that Force Majeure should not excuse a party from delay or failure in performing its obligations: 1) simply because performance has become commercially impracticable or more expensive or difficult; 2) where the failure to perform is due to the non-performing party's fault, negligence, or lack of diligence; or 3) where the party asserting Force Majeure fails to provide notice as required by the contract. Nor should Force Majeure apply as an excuse to performance unless the critical path for performance or delivery is actually affected. Thus it's not enough that there may have been a typhoon in the Sea of Japan unless the typhoon had a direct causal link that affected performance or delivery. The burden of demonstrating that causal link is on the party asserting the Force Majeure.

The contract should also recite that if a party is delayed or prevented from performing or becomes aware that it may be delayed or prevented from performing, due to the occurrence or anticipated occurrence of Force Majeure, the party asserting Force Majeure must:

(1) Use its best efforts to eliminate or circumvent Force Majeure. Contracts sometimes also state that it is understood that settlement of strike or other labor dispute shall be entirely at the discretion of the party affected thereby and that a subsequent finding of fault or culpability of the affected party with respect to the strike or labor dispute shall be immaterial to the treatment of such as an event of Force Majeure;

(2) Promptly, but not later than forty-eight (48) hours of the occurrence or anticipated occurrence of the Force Majeure, give the other party written notice of same, together with the expected duration of any Force Majeure and keep the other party currently informed as to the status of, or changes in circumstances or expected duration of said Force Majeure or anticipated Force Majeure.

(3) Promptly, but not later than [_____] ([__]) hours of when Force Majeure or the risk therein has been eliminated or has ceased to prevent the affected party from fulfilling its obligations; give the other party written notice of same, and

(4) Proceed to fulfill its obligations as soon as reasonably possible after such event of Force Majeure has been eliminated or has ceased to prevent the affected party from fulfilling such obligations.

Aside from defining what is meant by Force Majeure and specifying the notice requirements associated with a claim of Force Majeure, it's important to understand and anticipate how other parts of the contract may be affected by Force Majeure.

Cancellation and Termination

Note that deliveries which are not made during the period of Force Majeure must be deemed cancelled unless the parties enter into a formally executed written agreement rescheduling said delivery or deliveries. Typically, where a Force Majeure continues for more than [___] ([__]) days, either party may, at its option, terminate the Contract upon [___] ([__]) days advance written notice. Usually, in the event of cancellation or termination under the contract, neither party usually has any further responsibility or liability to the other.

ASSERTING WARRANTY CLAIMS

There are a few traps to avoid when making or dealing with warranties. First, suppliers or contractors may insert language in their confirming orders or contract documents that require claims to be made within a relatively short time after expiration of the warranty period (e.g. 90 days). This may seem benign but can have adverse consequences. Normally, the law gives you years in which to file a contractual claim for breach of warranty. This is called the statute of limitations. There is nothing illegal about shortening such a statute but instead of having years in which to file a claim you only have a relatively short period of time. It may take a while before the cause of something going wrong with a product or service is actually determined. Only agree to shorten the statute of limitations with a clear understanding of the risks and potential consequences. In addition, be mindful that most warranties run from the date a product or service is delivered or performed. Of course this can be changed by contract but if not it can lead to unintended consequences. For example, if goods are ordered and sit in a warehouse for an extended period of time before being placed into service, the warranty period may have elapsed before the goods are actually used.

When making or dealing with warranty claims ask the following questions:

1. What is the warranty's scope?
2. When does the warranty expire?

3. Was there a breach of warranty?
4. Was notice provided as required?
5. When does the remedy need to take place/be done?
6. What remedy applies to repaired or re-performed work?
7. How will the remedy affect cost/schedule or other work?
8. What is the value of the warranty work to be performed?
9. Were all important discussions and decisions documented?
10. Were subject matter experts and management kept apprised?
11. Does the contract permit "self-help" as a remedy and if so when?

Let's face it. Contract breaches are inevitable. Anticipate them and plan ahead. The key question to always ask yourself at the pre-contracting stage is "What is the remedy?" for a particular breach or failure to perform. This question forces you to face the inevitable and understand the consequences. Remember that contracts allow the parties to limit liability and available remedies (e.g. "repair or replace"). Very limited remedies with short warranty periods coupled with the exclusion of consequential damages or caps on liability (e.g. liquidated damages) can all operate to leave the Buyer in an unfavorable position in the event of a breach or other failure to perform. From the Buyer's perspective the follow-up question to ask is "Are there restrictions on exercising warranty rights." This might include the duty to provide notice or other hurdles as a pre-condition of exercising warranty rights. Parse the language. If the remedy entitles you to a replacement part does that part have to be "new" and if so what does "new" mean? Moreover, who is responsible for the associated removal and installation (i.e. "in and out costs")? Obviously, the time to think about and analyze remedies is early in the process and certainly before the contract is negotiated let alone signed. Remember also that the remedy can be and usually is a "price term" (i.e. a limited remedy) for a narrow or short warranty or the exclusion or limit on monetary damages can be "sold" to you as the "price" or a good "low-cost" deal. Be wary and get the best remedies you can given the risks and total lifecycle costs involved.

CLAIMS FOR EXTRAS

A key part of good contract management is having a clear protocol for dealing with changes. Not all changes constitute "extra work" justifying extra charges. This is an area where strong contract terms and conditions play a key role coupled with good contract administration and management. The possibility for changes, including extra work, needs to be not only anticipated but well managed as these issues arise. For example, if a supplier or contractor falls behind in the agreed upon schedule for delivery or performance and the buyer or owner requests that the supplier or contractor get back on schedule, this may generate a claim for extra compensation. Although this issue can be fact sensitive and case specific, telling a supplier or contractor who has fallen off schedule for through no fault of the buyer or owner does not necessarily justify extra compensation or time to perform.

When facing claims for extras ask the questions:

1. Was "extra" work performed?
2. Was "extra" work authorized?
3. Was notice provided as required?
4. Are the charges properly documented?
5. Will the "extra" work affect the schedule?

6. Was the "extra" work due to error or inefficiency?
7. Are the "extra" charges consistent with the contract?
8. Are certain of the charges barred by the contract terms?
9. Were all important discussions and decisions documented?
10. Were subject matter experts and management kept apprised?

DELAY CLAIMS

As in the case of claims for extras, not all claims for delays are compensable. A lot will depend on how the contract between the parties has allocated the risk of delays and whether the owner has bargained for (and indirectly paid for) contractual "no damage for delay" provisions. In any event, post execution management of delay claims is a key part of good contract management.

When facing delay (or Force Majeure) claims ask the following questions:

1. Did a delay occur?
2. What/who caused the delay?
3. How does the contract allocate risk of delay?
4. Were the notice requirements complied with?
5. Has supporting documentation been provided?
6. Could the delay have been avoided/mitigated?
7. Are the alleged damages correctly calculated?
8. Are the alleged damages barred by the contract?
9. Were subject matter experts and management kept apprised?
10. Were all important discussions and decisions documented?

Remember that good claims management begins with sound scope. It's also critically important to reserve the right to increase or decrease the scope of work or make other changes at some agreed upon pricing. These provisions should never be left up to "future agreement" or anticipated "mutual agreement". Nor are vague concepts such as changes will be determined based upon "equitable adjustments" wise given that perceptions may vary on what is just given the particular facts or circumstances.

PRICING ADJUSTMENT CLAUSES

Long-term contracts sometimes contain clauses which adjust the contract price over the course of time. The adjustment mechanisms are often called "escalation clauses". The better practice is to designate them as "adjustment clauses" since prices can be adjusted down as well as up. These clauses anticipate the effects of inflation or other factors affecting cost. Typically, this is done by tying price to some index.

Since escalation clauses can have unintended consequences, care needs to be taken in how they are structured. If the goods or services can be purchased on a fixed or cost-plus basis, the risk of an escalation clause can be avoided. Assuming that such pricing is not an option, the following points should be considered before agreeing to be bound by an escalation clause:

1) Secure the right to terminate the agreement.
2) Anticipate that market prices may decrease.
3) Specify how price adjustments will be made.
4) Specify when price adjustments will be made.
5) Clearly state any caps or limits on adjustments.
6) Specify the exact index or part (and base year).
7) Review all possible indexes which could be used.
8) Make a determination as to the best index to be used.

9) Ensure the index is related to what is being purchased.

10) Anticipate that an index may change or be discontinued.

11) Identify the applicable base price and specific date for same.

As noted above, an index for a particular transaction should be selected based on the type of project or procurement contemplated. Moreover, indices should be selected based on the type of cost being escalated since escalation indices represent group of items. For example, an escalation index for purchasing paper would be inappropriate for use with a cost estimate for a building project.

Cost indices have limitations since they are based on average data. Thus, judgment is required to decide if an index applies to a specific cost being updated. By carefully crafting escalation clauses to reflect the cost increases against which the seller should be protected, the risk of a "runaway" price escalation and overpayment by the purchaser, can be reduced.

Strong termination rights with the option to end the agreement on acceptable terms is another way a purchaser can protect itself against unanticipated consequences of escalation clauses. Termination rights are especially important when there is no cap on the escalation.

Usually only some component(s) of a purchase drive the need for an escalation clause. Ideally the index used reflects only those components. However, large indexes are often composites which may not have any real correlation to the particular component(s) that are driving the desire for an escalation clause. Moreover, just because an index has in the past, whether by coincidence or circumstance, had a correlation with price changes associated with a particular component, there is no guarantee that the correlation will continue. Where the price of one component has a disproportionate effect on total cost, an escalation clause predicated on a broadly based index will not reflect actual costs.

Since such clauses are designed to protect against long-term price changes, it may not make sense to have them apply immediately. Nor should such clauses protect the supplier against avoidable costs or costs already incurred. Consider placing limits on the escalation clause. The escalation could be made to apply only after a certain time or after costs have risen by a certain amount. It may not make sense to apply the escalation clause or the same index to all components of a procurement. Purchases involving a combination of both goods and services may warrant that different (or no) adjustments be made to certain components.

Note that if the contract contains a Force Majeure clause excusing performance under certain circumstances, it may be appropriate to reflect that the escalation provisions are tolled for the period of any Force Majeure.

ALTERNATIVES TO ESCALATION CLAUSES

1. **<u>A Cost-Plus Contract</u>** – is one alternative to using escalation clauses. Be sure to clearly and completely identify which costs are included and which cost components are to be reimbursed with fee and which at cost without markup. Also make sure that there are strong audit provisions in cost-plus contracts.

2. **<u>A Surcharge</u>** - is an addition to the price based on cost increases on one component. Such a surcharge could be based on actual cost or an applicable index. Most of the considerations applicable to escalation clauses are likewise applicable to surcharges, including how and when they are calculated and whether they reflect both price increases or decreases.

3. **<u>Option to Purchase</u>** – is the right, but not the obligation to buy at some set price. Usually, an option requires that consideration be paid for the right to buy in addition to the price to be paid for the goods or services to be purchased. By contrast, "firm offers" to sell <u>goods</u> are good for three months, without the need for any financial or other "consideration".

4. **<u>Increasing Prices</u>** – is the assumption that prices will continue to rise by some arbitrary amount. Simply agreeing to progressively higher prices might not make sense, since the prices set would not necessarily

reflect true cost or be competitive. Purchasers need to take the possibility of declining prices into consideration, and progressively higher pricing ignores that important aspect of a purchase. Also bear in mind that pricing can have an effect on a supplier's incentive to deliver at a particular time.

5. **Price Upon Delivery** – should only be used where it can be structured in such a way that the price is determined by competitive forces and not simply set by the supplier. Most "favored nations" provisions to the effect that pricing will not be less favorable than that offered to other customers for similar quantities offer some protection, but do not apply where the goods or services are designed to suit a particular purchaser's unique needs.

COMPENSATION CONCEPTS FOR TARGET PRICE CONTRACTS

Target Price contracts (i.e. contracts where the parties agree to share savings or costs above or below a specified target price based upon some allocation formula) are sometimes seen as a method of sharing risk between the buyer and the seller. It's important to understand that in Target Price contracts the key is the quality of the estimated cost of the work. It's clear therefore that target pricing is no substitute for a poorly defined scope of work which in turn drives the estimated cost of the work. In addition, a target price arrangement may have both fixed and target pricing arrangements as illustrated below:

1. The Contract Price for [PROJECT NAME] is $[_____] and consists of the Lump Sum Price of $[_____] and the Target Price of $[_____].

2. The above Contract Prices are intended to provide the Company with a high degree of budgetary certainty and reflect Contractor's commitment to achieve the Company's objectives on time and within budget. Toward that end, Contractor commits to minimize its requests for Changes under the Contract and to limit its Change Requests as specified herein.

3. For the Target Price portion of the Contract, Contractor will be compensated at full rates per Exhibit [____] up the Target Price. Beyond the Target Price, Company will be charged at Contractor's cost without profit up to 110% of the Target Price. Beyond 110% of the Target Price, Contractor will be compensated at full rates per Exhibit [____].

4. Contractor is entitled to earn an Incentive Fee in the event the Target Price is underrun and such Target Price Underrun shall be shared between the Parties on 60/40 percent basis, with 60% of the Target Price Underrun payable to the Company.

5. Changes to the Work will only increase the Target Price where the cost for out of scope work exceeds $[_____] per occurrence and such individual occurrence, and directly related costs, are documented by a Change Order Request demonstrating an increase in such cost and a Change Order is issued by the Company.

6. Changes to the Work will only increase the Lump Sum Price where the cost for the out of scope work exceeds $[____] per occurrence as specified above and is documented by a Change Order Request demonstrating an increase in the Indirect Costs and a Change Order is issued by the Company.

7. Indirect Costs means all costs related to indirect costs or expenses including construction equipment, home office support or charges, mobilization, health and safety (including HASP), insurance and credit guarantees, and indirect labor and supervision.

Bear in mind that target price contracts can be very challenging to administer and manage because so much time, effort and manpower resources has to be devoted to keeping an accurate track of what has been spent and by whom.

LIQUIDATED DAMAGES

Liquidated damages are popular but rarely understood. The best time to use them is rarely and carefully with a full understanding of their purpose and suitability for a particular transaction.

When To Use Liquidated Damages.

Where damages in the event of a breach would be difficult or impractical to ascertain and prove, parties to a contract are free to agree (stipulate) on a reasonable forecast of the damages for such a breach. These liquidated damages ("LDs") will be enforced if not grossly disproportionate to the damages that might reasonably be expected as a result of a breach.

What about "bonus" or incentive provisions?

Parties to a contract are also free to agree that a bonus or incentive payment will be made for early completion or some other performance beyond what is contractually required. However, just because you have LDs does not mean you must also include a bonus or incentive provision. LDs are compensation for breach. Bonuses are rewards for "extra" performance. You can have one without the other, or both.

The key aspects of liquidated damages.

LDs have the following basic aspects.

1. LDs do not eliminate the burden of establishing a breach.

2. LDs eliminate the cost and burden of proving the damages.

3. LDs act as a cap or limit of liability for the damages suffered.

4. LDs are appropriate when damages would be difficult to assess.

5. LDs must be compensatory, not punitive, since penalties are unenforceable. Do not refer to LDs as "penalties".

Seek Compensation, Not Punishment.

Contract law provides compensatory damages - not punishment - for breach of contract. You only get punitive damages where the other party's behavior is especially egregious and violates some duty other than a purely contractual one. If damages in the event of breach are readily ascertainable on the date of the contract, the court may view the LDs as a penalty.

Rules For Using Liquidated Damages.

LDs can be useful, but they should be used with care. Following these simple rules can help avoid problems.

1. Don't refer to LDs as "penalties".

2. Don't set LDs so high that they become "punitive".

3. Don't set LDs so low that they become an attractive "option" to breach.

4. Set LDs at an amount that is intended to be compensatory - a reasonable forecast of anticipated harm for a breach.

5. Remember that LDs will apply even if at the time of the breach the actual damages are higher or lower.

6. Consider how long LD payments will continue if the delay or deficiency is never corrected and whether they apply to non-performance.

7. Carefully coordinate LD provisions with any "bonus" or incentive clauses, as well as with other provisions of the contract to avoid conflicts or inconsistencies.

8. Make sure the LD provisions only apply to the damages you intend. For example, if a project completion date is not met, you may want to set LDs for the "loss of use" of the premises or completed work. This would leave you free to collect other damages such as for increased costs or expenses.

9. Anticipate that both parties may be at least partially at fault in the event of a breach. Some courts apportion LDs in delay cases. Some let the parties litigate the issue up to, but not to exceed the amount of the LDs. Other courts throw out the LDs ("all or none" rule) and let the parties litigate the issue of damages.

10. Consult with counsel. Liquidated damages and "bonus" or incentive provisions often result in disputes (finger pointing),

since the parties tend to blame each other if things go wrong. In addition, ambiguities are often strictly construed against the drafter. Make sure the LDs correctly reflect your intent.

Determining The Approach To Use.

LDs can be used broadly to cover any and all damages related to a breach or narrowly to apply to only certain types or portions of the associated damages. When used broadly, LDs operate to cap liability.

Determining The Dollar Amount of LDs.

LDs should be those which place the injured party in as good a monetary position as would have been enjoyed if performance had been rendered as promised. Consider using the rental or other costs of securing temporary goods or services, as well as associated administrative expenses. The figure used does not have to be an exact calculation, but it must be a reasonable forecast of the harm. The amount can be expressed as either a specific dollar amount (e.g., $1,000.00) or a sum certain (e.g., ten percent of the Contract Price).

The Common Law And The UCC Approaches.

The common-law (general) rule is that LDs must be a reasonable forecast of the anticipated harm for breach. What if the LDs are not a reasonable forecast when set, but turn out to be at the time of breach? The general rule is that such LDs would be held to be unenforceable. By contrast, the Uniform Commercial Code (Section 2-718) applicable to sales transactions predominantly involving goods takes the approach that LDs will be enforced if reasonable in light of either "anticipated" or "actual" harm.

LDs Compared To Limitation Of Liability Clauses.

Under a limitation of liability ("LOL") clause, damages, (not merely breach) must be proved, and liability varies according to the extent of the injury up to the stated maximum. Unlike LDs, it is immaterial whether the LOL is a reasonable estimate of probable damages in the event of a breach. Nor is a LOL a penalty, since it does not operate to punish for breach.

Must The Non-Breaching Party "Mitigate" Its LDs?

No. One of the rules of contract law is that in the event of a breach, the non-breaching party must take reasonable steps to minimize and not to increase ("mitigate") its damages. However, LDs contemplate the inability to ascertain damages. Nor does collecting LDs increase one's damages. Thus, there is no duty to "mitigate" LDs.

Use LDs Defensively To Limit Liability.

Since LDs operate as a cap on liability, they can be used to minimize and control risks. For example, software licenses often contain strict clauses prohibiting making copies. What happens if a copy is inadvertently made? LDs could be used to specify that unauthorized copies would be made at 110% of list price or some other sum certain, thereby limiting the licensee's liability to a predictable amount.

LDs Based On Performance Shortfalls.

LDs can be made applicable to performance shortfalls in either service or goods. For example, where equipment fails to perform as specified by contract, LDs can be used to address the deficiency or shortfall. Be sure to specify that the LDs are payable in the event of a failure to achieve an agreed upon performance level and are not excused due to so-called "temporary" failures because of warranty repairs. In service contracts, LDs can be tied to response time or productivity.

Does A Performance Bond Cover LDs?

Where a performance bond, either directly or by implication, incorporates the underlying contract by reference, the surety is liable for any LDs owed by the contractor. Avoid disputes. Make sure the bond states that the underlying contract is incorporated into and made a part of the bond.

Incentives Based On Contract Compliance.

Resist the suggestion to provide incentive payments in addition to the contract price simply to perform as promised. Incentives should be designed to cover "extra" performance above and beyond what the other party is already obligated to do by contract.

Can You Collect LDs If You Caused The Breach Or Delay?

No. However, the contract can provide that Company caused delays will operate as an extension of time, but that the contractor will still be liable for LDs due to his or her breach or unexcused delay.

What If The Supplier Fails To Provide Notice Of Delay?

Contracts often provide that if the contractor believes that the owner has caused a delay, the contractor must provide prompt written notice. Suppose the owner causes delay, but the contractor fails to give notice as required. Does this owner get LDs? No, but the contractor could not collect delay damages.

Is A Take-or-pay Clause A Type Of LDs?

No. A take-or-pay contract simply provides two alternative methods of performance: take (and pay) or pay. The buyer is guaranteed a certain supply and the seller is assured a steady market. Since the contract can be performed in either manner, there is no breach, and the principles applicable to LDs do not apply.

LDs As A Permissive Measure Of Damages.

Where LDs are the sole and exclusive remedy for breach, they establish the upper limit of recovery and preclude the non-breaching party from pursuing any other damages. Could a party retain the option to either recover liquidated damages or seek its actual damages? It depends.

Some courts allow the parties to make LDs permissive or "optional" simply by using the word "may" or "optional". Other courts take the position that there is no such thing as optional LDs, since if LDs are optional, they are not "liquidated" and operate as unenforceable penalty. Check the law of the applicable jurisdiction.

Retaining The Right To Specific Performance.

Particularly in cases involving specially manufactured goods, orders with long lead times or transactions involving real property, you may want to retain your right to specific performance in addition to LDs. Check with counsel to see whether this is possible under the law of the applicable jurisdiction. Particularly in the case of specific performance, courts may view the right to delivery and possession of unique goods or real estate contracted for as fundamentally different and distinct from monetary damages for breach of the contract. Of course, parties can waive their right to specific performance by making the LDs the sole and exclusive remedy.

Consider How The Other Contract Clauses Will Affect LDs.

You can't collect LDs for delays which are "excusable" under the contract because of owner-ordered changes in the work, owner-caused delays, or agreed upon "force majeure" excuses. Nor can you collect LDs in excess of any limitations of liability ("LOL") clause. If LDs are payable upon termination for cause, consider what constitutes "cause" or "material" breaches. Also bear in mind that the contract's choice of law provision can affect how the LDs will be interpreted and applied.

Specific Applications Of Liquidated Damages.

As previously indicated, LDs can be used to address late or non-delivery, late or non-performance, as well as failure to perform as specified by contract. Consider the following three scenarios (or any combination thereof) involving a contract for the purchase and installation of equipment or the provision of services.

Late or non-delivery

Late or improper installation/performance

Performance deficiencies or shortfalls (output, power, efficiency, reliability, productivity, or the like)

How could LDs be structured to address these risks?

Sample Liquidated Damage Clauses.

A simple LD clause might read:

"The Parties agree that in the event of [ ], the Seller shall pay Buyer liquidated damages of [$] per [ ], given that the harm to Buyer would be very difficult or impracticable to calculate and that the amount fixed as liquidated damages is not a penalty, but a reasonable forecast of just compensation for said harm."

Consider the following more complex LD clauses. Naturally, any clause would need to be tailored to fit the specifics of the individual case.

Sample Liquidated Damages Clause For Late Delivery Of Equipment.

1. The Delivery Date for the Equipment is.

2. Seller shall pay Buyer liquidated damages of $_if the Equipment is not delivered on or before the Delivery Date, provided, however, that actual delivery shall not be made earlier than five (5) calendar days before the Equipment Delivery Date.

3. Additional liquidated damages of $_for each calendar day that the Equipment is delivered after the Delivery Date up to a maximum of ninety (90) calendar days shall be paid to the Company.

4. The liquidated damages are not a penalty, but a reasonable forecast of the damages to which they apply, given that said damages would be very difficult to assess.

5. If the Equipment is not delivered within ten (10) days of the Delivery Date, Buyer shall have the right to cancel its order for the Equipment without any obligation or liability to Seller.

6. Seller shall provide five (5) calendar days prior written notice of Seller's intention to deliver on any day other than the Delivery Date, and said date must be acceptable to the Buyer.

7. In addition to liquidated damages as provided hereunder, Buyer shall have the right to compel specific performance of this Agreement, including the delivery of the Equipment.

Sample Liquidated Damages Clause For Late Performance With Optional Early Completion Incentive Provision.

1. The Completion Date for the Work is.

2. For each and every full calendar day that the Work is completed before the Completion Date, the Contractor shall be entitled to a bonus of $_per day as an incentive payment up to a maximum amount of $.

3. For each calendar day that the Work is completed after the Completion Date, the Company shall be entitled to a payment of $_per day as liquidated damages due to the Company's loss of use of those portions of the Work that were not completed by the Completion Date, as well as the diminished use of the Completed Work and the Company's premises, up to a maximum amount of $.

4. The liquidated damages are not a penalty, but a reasonable forecast of the damages to which they apply, given that said damages would be very difficult to assess.

5. The Work shall be deemed completed when the Contract shall have been fully and completely performed. Under no

circumstances shall partial, substantial, or less than full and complete performance of the Work on the Completion Date entitle the Contractor to any bonus as an incentive payment.

6. Delays, if any, which affect the Completion Date shall be handled, as set forth in Article of the Contract. Delays caused by the Company will operate as an extension of time, but Contractor shall still be liable for delays caused by Contractor.

7. The Company's Project Manager shall be the sole arbiter of whether or not the Contractor or the Company are entitled to any incentive payment or liquidated damages, as provided herein and his or her good-faith determination, decision, and judgment shall be final, binding, and conclusive on the Parties.

Sample Liquidated Damage Clause For Equipment Performance Warranty Shortfall

1. If the performance of the Equipment as demonstrated by the Performance Test is less than that specified in Performance Warranty, Contractor shall, within thirty (30) days of said Performance Test, take all actions necessary to achieve the Performance Warranty.

2. If, within thirty (30) calendar days of the Performance Tests the Equipment fails to meet the Performance Warranty, Contractor shall be liable to the Company for liquidated damages for failure to achieve the Performance Warranty, as set forth below:

CRITERIA	SHORTFALL DOLLAR AMOUNT
Output	
Power	
Efficiency	
Reliability	
Productivity	
Other	

3. Said liquidated damages shall be due to the Company as a result of the failure to achieve the Performance Warranty, and the liquidated damages are not a penalty, but a reasonable forecast of the damages to the Company for failure to achieve the Performance Warranty, given that said damages would be very difficult to assess.

4. The Performance Test shall be that specified in Attachment of the Contract.

5. The Performance Warranty shall be the guaranteed performance level as specified in Attachment of the Contract.

Sample Liquidated Damages Clause For Unauthorized Inadvertent Copying.

The Company shall not make copies of the software except as permitted by this Agreement. In the event that through the Company's inadvertence, unauthorized copies are made, then for each such copy, the Company shall pay Licensor the sum of $_($) Dollars as liquidated damages, not as a penalty, but as a reasonable forecast of the Licensor's damages, given that said damages would be very difficult to assess. In the event that the unauthorized copies are made due to the Company's intentional or deliberate misconduct, the liquidated damages shall not apply, and the Licensor shall be entitled to recover its direct damages.

Sample Liquidated Damages Clause For Breach of Contract.

If the sale contemplated by this Agreement is not consummated as a result of a breach of this Agreement, then the breaching party shall pay the non-breaching party the sum of $_($) Dollars as liquidated damages, not as a penalty, but as a reasonable forecast of the non-breaching party's damages in the event that the sale is not consummated, given that such damages would be very difficult to assess.

LIMITATIONS OF LIABILITY CLAUSES

The Right to Compensatory Damages

The law says that in the event of a breach of contract, the injured party can collect all the monetary damages that result from the breach as compensation. These compensatory damages include both direct as well as indirect (consequential) damages. The law also says that parties are usually free to limit commercial risk by using contractual limitations of liability clauses. As a result, contract clauses limiting liability are quite common.

Key Aspects of Limitations of Liability Clauses

A limitation of liability clause is probably the single most important clause in any contract. It limits a party's liability to a specific amount or type of damage. Limitations of liability typically have two basic components. They limit damages to some set amount (e.g., the contract price or some multiple thereof) and exclude certain types of damages such as consequential damages (e.g., loss of profits, revenues, efficiency, or the like).

Key Considerations Re Limitations of Liability Clauses

Contractors, consultants and other suppliers of goods or services routinely include limitations of liability clauses in their contracts or request that the purchaser's limitation of liability be made applicable to both parties. Although a supplier's desire to limit its liability is understandable, that limitation of liability should obviously not be less than at least the contract price. This provides the supplier with the appropriate incentive to perform. **Moreover, a limitation of liability clause should not limit the supplier's obligation to defend or indemnify the purchaser, nor affect the supplier's insurance obligations, as provided for under the contract.**

How to Structure Limitations of Liability Clauses

What if the contract price is very low or what if within a given contractual transaction the price can vary from a few to millions of dollars per order? Or, what if the price is not yet known as is often the case with "blanket order" or "general services" agreements? In such cases, the supplier's liability can be limited to the <u>greater</u> of some multiple (say three times (3x) the value of the order) or $250,000 or some other such dollar figure. This gives the seller enough of a "stake" in the transaction, protects the purchaser, and still avoids open-ended liability for consequential damages.

Sample Pro-Purchaser Limitation of Liability Clause

The intent should be to preserve the supplier's incentive to perform, as well as the purchaser's indemnity and insurance protection. Ensuring that the purchaser is properly protected (where the purchaser wants to give up its right to consequential damages) can be done by using the following simple language. This language assumes that the purchaser's liability is limited under a separate clause.

> <u>LIMITATION OF LIABILITY</u>
> The [Supplier's, Contractor's, Consultant's, etc. . .] total liability to the Company for all claims or suits of any kind, whether based upon contract, tort (including negligence),

warranty, strict liability, or otherwise, for any losses, damages, costs or expenses of any kind whatsoever arising out of, resulting from, or related to the performance or breach of this Contract shall, under no circumstances, exceed three times or $250,000.00, whichever is greater, the contract price, as may be amended by agreed upon price for extra work authorized by written change order.

The Parties [or their contractors, subcontractors, or suppliers of any tier] shall not, in any circumstances, be liable for any special, indirect, incidental, punitive, or consequential losses, damages, costs, or expenses whatsoever (including, but not limited to, lost or reduced profits, revenues, efficiency, bonding capacity, or business opportunities, or increased or extended overhead, operating, maintenance or depreciation costs and expenses).

NOTWITHSTANDING ANYTHING TO THE CONTRARY, THIS LIMITATION OF LIABILITY SHALL IN NO EVENT AFFECT OR APPLY TO CONTRACTOR'S OBLIGATIONS WITH REGARD TO DEFENSE, INDEMNIFICATION, OR INSURANCE AS PROVIDED FOR UNDER THIS CONTRACT.

Incidental Damages

Although it may be reasonable to agree to limit a supplier's liability to a multiple of the contract price, waiving one's rights to "incidental damages" should only be rarely agreed to. The reason is that incidental damages are any reasonable expenses incurred by the purchaser incident to the supplier's breach. Incidental damages include expenses incurred by the purchaser in the receipt, inspection, transportation, care, and custody of goods rightfully rejected as nonconforming to the contract. Incidental damages also include any reasonable charges, expenses, or commissions in connection with obtaining substitute goods to replace nonconforming goods. Since incidental damages are related to expenses incurred as a direct result of a breach and are not uncertain or unlimited like consequential damages, there is no overwhelming need to exclude such damages.

Time to Sue Limitations

Some limitations of liability require that any claim or suit be filed against the contractor within a specified period of time such as one year. Although it may be reasonable for a purchaser to require that any claims or suits for alleged payments owed be filed within one year of the work being performed in order to bring closure to a particular project or transaction, it doesn't necessarily make sense to make this requirement applicable to the purchaser since this could negatively impact on its warranty rights which often exceed one year in duration. Therefore, the purchaser should not contractually agree to shorten the "statute of limitations", i.e., the time the purchaser has to file suit for breach.

The typical statute of limitations for the purchase of goods is four years, while the statute of limitations applicable to transactions where the "service" component predominates is usually six years. This means that a purchaser has either four or six years, depending on the nature of the transaction, to file suit for any breach of contract which occurred during the applicable warranty period.

Choice of Law and Venue

Since different jurisdictions may apply slightly different standards regarding the enforceability of limitation of liability clauses, it's important to factor that into the contract's choice of law provision. Note that parties may elect to have the law of a certain state or jurisdiction (e.g. New York or England) apply to their transaction and still specify a different venue (e.g. Chicago or Tokyo) dictating the location where any disputes will be heard and resolved. Choice of law alone does not necessarily dictate where a case will be heard. The time available to sue can vary depending on the contract's choice of law provisions. That is another reason why choice of law provisions are important. When it comes to venue, "home court" is typically an advantage for a variety of reasons not the least of which is convenience.

KEY CONTRACT MANAGEMENT PRACTICES

The following key contract management practices will help ensure you've got the best possible contracts and that they are managed efficiently. These practices can be integrated into a clear and complete Contract Management Plan ("CMP") tailored to the individual transaction.

1. Get The Best Warranties You Can

A warranty is a promise, made as part of a contract, that a particular fact is true. Samples, models, representations, statements, presentations, pictures, proposals, descriptions, catalogues, literature, or the like can all be sources of warranties if they are made a basis of the bargain. In commercial transactions, the parties are free to negotiate whatever warranties they like and may create, modify, or disclaim warranties.

Warranty provisions are among the most important contractual terms and conditions in any agreement and one should guard against losing warranty rights by providing notice of breach and reserving your rights.

Remember that the law lets you write your own warranties. Chances are that if you do not have good warranties, it's your own fault. When analyzing or negotiating warranties, consider the following:

1. When do the warranties begin?

2. How long do the warranties last?

3. What are the remedies for breach?

4. Are the warranties clearly expressed?

5. What implied warranties, if any, apply?

6. What conditions, disclaimers or limitations apply?

7. Have all important promises that were made been incorporated into the agreement?

8. Have you avoided making warranties (express or implied) which you did not intend to make?

9. Do the warranties address the cost of access to the defective goods or the cost of correcting other work made bad due to the "defective" work?

2. Know The UCC Warranties

The UCC applies to the sale of Goods or sometimes where goods and services are both being purchased, especially where the sale of goods "predominates" the transaction. Essentially, the UCC warranties are:

1. Warranty of Title

   • Good title

2. Warranty of no liens or encumbrances

   • No security interests or the like

3. Warranty of No Infringement

   • Goods do not infringe

   (Inapplicable where buyer specifies design)

4. Express Warranties

   • Verbal or written

   • Statements or representations

5. Warranty of Merchantability

   • Pass without objection in the trade

   • Fit for general or usual purpose

   • Fair average quality within description

6. Warranty of Fitness

   • Fit for a particular purpose

- Seller knows the particular purpose

- Buyer relies on seller's skill or judgment to select or furnish goods for the intended purpose.

3. Know The Common Law Warranties

- Implied warranties – generally the Common Law does not reflect many implied warranties.

- Express warranties – the Common Law generally allows parties to craft their own warranties as reflected by contract.

4. Watch Out for the Inventory Time Bomb

Warranties are judged by their scope (what is covered) and duration (when they start and end). Be sure your warranty is broad enough to cover your needs. For example, if you typically inventory goods for a year or more, your warranty may run out while the product is "on the shelf." That is because warranties on goods typically start to run upon delivery, not upon use or incorporation into the work. Also make sure that repairs or replacements are themselves warranted for an acceptable period of time.

5. Make A Careful Selection.

Even if you are buying mass-produced goods which are uniform and indistinguishable from one another, services for various suppliers can be quite personal and individualized. Request and check references and get positive recommendations from former customers. Remember that although a firm's reputation is important, individuals will be working on the matter. Look for experience, knowledge, and compatibility.

6.   Define The Scope of Work To Be Performed.

Make sure the scope of work clearly and completely sets forth what is to be done. The scope or statement of work should specify all the duties and responsibilities including all work necessary to accomplish the project. If a high percentage of procurement transactions are "change orders", it suggests the possibility of poor scope of work documents or lack of aggressive contract administration and contract measures. Develop some internal guidelines as to what constitutes a "good" scope of work.

7.   Specify The Deliverables To Be Provided.

Specify the deliverables to be provided, including such details as the number, due date, and the like. One can specify that the deliverables will be in accordance with a particular model, sample, layout, or format.

8.   Specify Where The Services Will Be Provided Or Goods Delivered.

It is useful to specify the location where the professional services will be performed in terms of a particular location or locations. Where the services will be provided may have an impact of both the direct and indirect cost of the services. Address where the goods are to be delivered and who has the risk of loss in transit. Don't rely on "FOB" abbreviations. Spell out who exactly is on the risk of loss in transit.

9.   Set The Standards Governing Performance.

Set performance standards for goods or requirements and make sure they will meet operating requirements. Professionals are usually expected to perform their services with the care, skill, and diligence in accordance with the applicable and currently recognized professional standards. That standard may or may not fit every need and is expressed in highly generalized terms. If a higher or more objective standard is required, it should be articulated.

10. Specify The Objectives To Be Achieved.

Absent a guarantee of specific results, those engaged in professions are held only to the standards generally followed in their particular profession and are required only to exercise due care. They may, of course, be held for malpractice or negligent performance. However, the parties can agree to specific guarantees or that a particular result will be accomplished. Basically, pay for performance - not promises.

11. Specify The Ownership Of Work Product.

All the results of the work, including deliverables, should be the property of the purchaser. Specify in a signed written contract that the deliverables are "works made for hire" and that you own not only the tangible deliverables themselves, but also that all intellectual property rights, such as copyright or patent rights, are assigned to the purchaser. At a minimum, secure an irrevocable royalty-free license to unrestricted use of the deliverables within your organization.

12. Identify Key Personnel, As Appropriate.

If applicable, specify the individuals who will be providing the services. If those particular individuals are absolutely indispensable, the agreement can be made contingent upon their involvement. If their participation is not indispensable, the agreement can specify that their employer will use its best efforts to ensure that they are available to work on the project. Anticipate that individuals sometimes change employers and how this could affect the contract or project. Is this a cause for termination by either party? Also, if you specify an individual and you are then dissatisfied with the work, you may be in an awkward position.

13. Consider Availability.

Sometimes it may be appropriate to engage the services of a firm or professional on an exclusive basis for a specified period of time. If the services are provided on an exclusive basis, those services cannot be provided to others during the period specified. If the services are not to be provided on an exclusive basis, the agreement may specify that the services will be provided on a nonexclusive, but "first priority" basis. You may have to pay a premium for first priority, but it will help ensure availability.

14. Request Proposals.

Suppliers should prepare a comprehensive proposal reflecting the purchaser's needs and requirements. Proposals should include a clear statement of the objective(s) sought to be achieved, along with a comprehensive scope of work. The approach to be followed, including the project stages and sequence of work, should be covered. Staffing and availability, along with qualifications and references, should also be provided. Naturally, proposals should include details on time to complete and cost of the work.

Requiring proposals promotes competition and makes it a "horse race". It is also a first step away from excessive "sole" or "single" sourcing.

15. Determine the Supplier's Accountability.

Some suppliers such as architects and engineers, provide the owner with a plan, design, or other such work product which will have a direct impact on the project. Likewise, a construction manager or design builder can commit to accomplish an objective. By contrast, a consultant may, depending on the assignment, only provide ideas or recommendations with the owner retaining accountability and responsibility. Determine what level accountability will be imposed on the professional. The key is whether you are contracting for specific results or merely for effort.

16. Secure Protection From Infringement Claims.

Services often take the form of expressions of an idea or application of a process. Copyright law protects authors of original works against use by any other party. Patent holders have the right to exclusive use, or to deny others the use, of their inventions. Legal protection is also available for trade secrets. Therefore, the parties should address the risk of claims or suits premised upon actual or alleged infringement. Usually, the purchaser is entitled to broad indemnification protection against such suits or claims by third parties.

17. Specify That The Supplier May Not Assign
    The Agreement To a Third Party.

The personal nature of many, if not most, services makes it imperative that the purchaser be able to choose who will be providing the services. Therefore, the agreement should specify that the supplier cannot assign its duties or responsibilities to any third party without the prior written consent of the purchaser.

Such clauses typically state that said consent "shall not be unreasonably withheld." That may create a triable fact issue and thereby land you in court. One possible compromise is to allow the supplier the right to assign "rights" (e.g., the right to be paid), but not to assign "obligations" (e.g., the duty to perform). Watch out because under such an approach the supplier could "assign" its right to sue the buyer to some third party (e.g., a subcontractor or supplier).

18. Avoid Making Unwise Commitments To
    Provide Manpower Or Other Resources.

It is often tempting to promise to contribute equipment, facilities, manpower, or other resources to assist the supplier of professional services in fulfilling its responsibilities. If those resources are not provided in accordance with expectations, the supplier may assert that its failure to perform is attributable to the purchaser. Generally, it is safest to limit the buyer's obligations to paying money or to specify that there is no guarantee that such support will be provided.

19. Avoid Liability For Delays.

Smaller firms with fewer employees and less structured procedures may expect very quick turnaround for decisions or document review. Only agree to review drafts, plans, specifications, or other deliverables under a timetable which is acceptable. Consider a "no-damage-for-delay" clause permitting time extensions, but no additional money due to delays. The time extension should equal the period of the delay and apply to delays caused by either party or unforeseen events.

20. Disclaim Liability To Third Party Users.

If the work product or other deliverables are to be used or relied upon by third parties, the information should be supplied with appropriate disclaimers specifying that the data is being supplied for informational purposes only and is not guaranteed by the Company. Such disclaimers should be "CONSPICUOUS" (i.e., in type that is bold, larger, or otherwise "stands out".)

21. Know when the UCC Does Not Apply.

Generally speaking, if you have a contract the UCC does not apply except in limited situations. The UCC is essentially a "gap" filling device that applies where the parties are buying goods and have an incomplete agreement. There are some of aspects of the UCC that cannot be disclaimed such as "good faith" but generally parties are free to structure the deal and allocate the risks as they see fit.

Where the purchase of services predominates, the transaction is governed by the "common law", not the Uniform Commercial Code ("UCC"). The provisions of the UCC which provide certain implied warranties do not automatically apply to the purchase of professional services. If the implied warranties of merchantability and fitness for a particular purpose are to apply, they must specifically be stated in the contract. In addition, services should be purchased via a written contract signed by both parties, rather than by an exchange of purchase orders. Unwritten or unsigned contracts containing provisions for insurance or indemnification may be difficult to enforce. Also, an assignment of copyright ownership must be in writing and signed.

22. Avoid Making Any Implied Warranties.

If you cannot guarantee site access on a specific date or the accuracy of information or specifications you give to the supplier, be sure to "CONSPICUOUSLY" specify that access will depend on operating requirements and that any data is being provided for informational purposes only.

23. Specify Independent Contractor Status.

The relationship between the buyer and supplier should be clearly defined (e.g. owner-contractor, buyer-seller, etc. . . .). Particularly in the case where individuals will be providing services for an extended period of time, care should be taken to avoid creating an unintended employee-employer relationship.

24. Preserve Independent Contract Status.

Another reason to create and preserve "independent contractor" status is that as a general rule one who hires a contractor is not liable for the contractor's negligence. By contrast, employers or principals may be held liable for the negligence of their employees or agents. However, an owner can be held liable for the contractor's negligence if: 1) the work is a nuisance or inherently dangerous, 2) the owner controls how the work is to be performed, or 3) an incompetent contractor is hired. An owner can also be held liable for a contractor's negligence if the owner allows the contractor to become the owner's actual or apparent agent.

25. Avoid Tax, Employment, Or Benefit Liability.

Whether a supplier is an independent contractor or an employee has significant tax consequences for both the individual and the Company. Under the law, an employer is required to withhold and/or pay a part of income, social security, and unemployment taxes. An independent contractor pays its own taxes. Employees also have certain statutory rights (including the right to benefits or to unionize) which do not apply to independent contractors.

26. Seek Appropriate Indemnification Protection.

Decide what level of risk you are willing to accept, given the nature of the transaction and obtain indemnification protection commensurate with that risk. Of course, a promise to indemnify is only good if the one making the promise is solvent or has contractual liability insurance. Get a guarantee from the parent company, if possible, if the subsidiary you are dealing with is poorly financed. It costs nothing, but gives a lot of protection. It is also easy to do. Simply add a sentence to the contract that the parent guarantees the subsidiary's performance and add the parent as a signatory or get the parent to provide the guarantee in a separate document.

27. Know The Indemnification Basics.

Case law holds that one cannot be indemnified for one's own negligence unless the contract "unequivocally" indicates such an intent. In addition, in some states you cannot be indemnified for bodily injury or property damage due to one's sole negligence. However, under that statute, one can be one hundred percent (100%) indemnified if one is ninety-nine percent (99%) (or less) negligent. By contrast, other state statutes take a stricter view by precluding indemnification where a party is even partially at fault. This is a case where choice of law makes a difference. Anti-indemnification statutes may not apply to financial loss (e.g., lost profits) or defense costs. A contractual duty to defend can be triggered by a claim or suit, while the duty to indemnify can be triggered by a loss or liability. Finally, most anti-indemnity statutes do not apply to situations that are not related to bodily injury.

28. Obtain Appropriate Audit Provisions.

Where the supplier is to be compensated on a time and materials or cost-plus basis, the purchaser should have the right to audit the supplier's records. Auditors also like to be able to review travel and entertainment records that relate to expenses incurred in connection with the buyer's employees.

29. Protect Confidential Information.

Suppliers often have the need for or access to information which is confidential, sensitive, or proprietary to the purchaser of the professional services. Accordingly, appropriate confidentiality and nondisclosure provisions may be necessary in order to protect such information against unauthorized use.

30. Avoid Clauses Which Overly Restrict The
    Ability To Recover Damages Or Losses.

Since the purchaser's obligation is essentially limited to paying money, it may be appropriate to limit the purchaser's liability to the contract price. However, agreeing to limit the supplier's liability to the fee to be paid may not provide the purchaser with sufficient protection, particularly if the fee is relatively low compared to the risks. Consider a multiple of the contract price (e.g., 3x) or $500,000.00, whichever is greater, as a compromise.

31. Avoid Unwanted Publicity.

Suppliers of services often want to publicize the fact that a particular company or institution is utilizing their services and include such information in various promotional materials. The agreement can specify that the purchaser's name and identifying characteristics, will not be included in any promotional materials without the purchaser's prior written consent.

32. Seek Protection Against Lien Claims.

Some state statutes allow certain suppliers to file liens against the purchaser's real estate in the case of nonpayment. This right can also extend to subcontractors and suppliers. Determine whether a waiver of lien claims is appropriate or whether the supplier can agree to indemnify the purchaser against liens filed by the supplier's subcontractors or suppliers.

33. Get A Personal Satisfaction Guarantee.

If the supplier promises you that all work will be to your complete satisfaction, you need to consider the nature of the work to know what the effect of such a personal satisfaction warranty. If there is an objective "right way" of doing something and the professional performs the work in the right way, you cannot reject the work for any reason just because of the promise of personal satisfaction. You must have at least a reasonable objective basis for your dissatisfaction. On the other hand, if the deliverables are more in the nature of "art", beauty, or involves questions of personal preference, your opinion will generally govern, provided you are acting in good faith.

34. Identify, Evaluate, And Allocate The Risks.

High-risk transactions include situations where the deliverables are ill-defined, where the parties have never worked together before, and where the potential for damages, loss, or injury is high. Some transactions involve relatively few risks. A "paper study" conducted off premises may have very low risk. By contrast, an environmental or technical assessment present greater risks. Analyze risk in terms of both probability (high-low) and consequences (serious - not serious).

35. Include Standard Protective Clauses.

Choosing the law applicable to the transaction, picking the place where disputes will be litigated, limiting the purchaser's liability to the contract price, securing the right to make changes, specifying the period during which any suit may be filed, and securing appropriate indemnification, insurance provisions, and other contract rights are important in all transactions.

36. Maintain Control Over Costs.

Consider contracting for services for a Guaranteed Maximum Price ("GMP") on the basis of lump sum, time and materials, or cost-plus fee not to exceed the amount specified as the GMP. The transaction can also be based on an "estimate" not to exceed a "ceiling" amount. As an alternative, some portion of the work could be performed on a T&M basis, while other deliverables might be provided at a fixed price. Open-ended fees with no limit on the maximum number of hours or dollar amount can be a problem. Also bear in mind that the longer a project continues, the more expensive it tends to be. Keep things moving along.

37. Specify Your Policy On Expenses.

Most companies have rules or policies regarding travel or other business-related expenses. Suppliers of services who incur such expenses and expect to pass those expenses along to their clients should agree to comply with their client's rules or guidelines or reimbursement for such expenses. Also, specify whether time spent traveling is billable.

38. Specify Which Expenses Are Reimbursable
     At Cost Without Fee.

Some items should be provided to the purchaser at cost, particularly in cost-plus fee contracts. Taxes, fees paid to subcontractors on cost-plus work, permit or license fees, insurance premiums, travel expenses and accommodations, photocopying, telephone, telegraph, postage, messenger services, and the like should not be "profit centers" and should be passed along without markup.

39. Require A Schedule And Project End Date.

In the case of a complex undertaking, a schedule indicating how and when the work sequence will be performed may be useful in keeping the project on track. Periodic progress reports and meetings should be specified. Those in attendance at project meetings should be required to voice any scheduling problems at that meeting or lose the right to complain about any delay. Specifying the "end point" of the undertaking can also help focus the effort. An agreed upon date when the project will end or deliverables will be due can be useful.

40. Address Potential Conflicts Of Interest.

The agreement should reflect that the supplier warrants that there are no present, past, or future commitments or obligations which would place the supplier in a conflict of interest situation or, if appropriate, that steps have been taken to avoid a conflict of interest situation. A conflict of interest can arise where the supplier is forced with having to choose between the competing interests of different clients. Even the appearance of impropriety should be avoided.

41. Require Coordination and Reporting.

Sometimes an individual contract may have to be completed within the context of overall project objectives. This may require the supplier to coordinate its activities with those of others including other suppliers. In addition, the supplier should keep the purchaser continually informed as to project scheduling, status, and costs.

42. Specify Responsibility For Training,
    Certification, and Licensing.

It may be appropriate to specify that the supplier will be responsible to ensure that all persons providing services contracted for shall be properly trained and qualified by education and experience and that the supplier is responsible for all training, certification, and licensing requirements.

43. Identify Joint Authors.

Copyright law protects an author's expression against unauthorized reproduction. Unless otherwise agreed, an employer usually owns works of authorship made in the scope of employment. By contrast, one who hires an independent contractor does not automatically own the copyright. Copyright should be transferred by signed agreement. Also bear in mind that where two or more persons make independent contributions that could each stand alone as original works of authorship, both have a copyright interest and assignments are required from all authors.

44. Watch Out For Finger Pointing.

In a complex undertaking, the buyer may find that the contractors, consultant, architect, engineer, project manager, and others are blaming each other and the purchaser itself for problems, delays, or inefficiencies. A clearly drafted agreement can reduce the risks associated with this type of situation. Designating one individual with lead responsibility (e.g., design-builder) can focus accountability. So can requiring "coordination of effort" among the various suppliers, well-drafted scope and sequence of work provisions, and clearly articulated deliverables. Advanced planning, proper management, and attention to project scheduling can also help keep the project on track.

45. Watch Out For Assertions Of
    Ownership In An Idea.

Given the nature of ideas or concepts which exist in the mind as thoughts or mental images, the law does not usually allow individuals to assert a proprietary interest in them. However, the law recognizes that if in consideration of disclosure an individual agrees to pay someone for an idea or to keep an idea confidential, that promise can be enforced, particularly if the idea is unique or original. Generally speaking, the unrestricted use of ideas or concepts should be preserved. Litigation in this area is growing. Consider using a good "form letter" for responding to unsolicited offers to disclose an "idea" in exchange for a percentage of the "savings".

46. Watch Out For Unknown Deliverables.

Special care needs to be taken when contracting for deliverables which are experimental or prototypical. For example, in a software development contract, it may be difficult to clearly define the end product. In such situations, purchasers typically seek to contract for a result (i.e., a program), whereas the supplier may seek to limit responsibility to merely providing services on a "best efforts" basis. These contradictory objectives may result in a vague agreement.

47. Recognize The Design Professional's Liabilities.

Liability For Work Product

Although the common law standard of care applicable to professionals is somewhat vague, professionals are liable for their acts of professional negligence. Whether a professional has departed from the standard of care generally followed by others in the profession can be a highly subjective and case-specific determination.

Liability For Approval

In addition to providing design, a professional also may recommend or approve materials, products, or components which are to be incorporated into the work or project, but which the design professional did not design. If the owner is relying on the design professional's skill, experience, and expertise, the professional can be held liable for failing to properly investigate the suitability of what has been recommended or approved.

Liability For Acts Of Others

Naturally, a design professional is also liable to the owner if the services of the design professional's subcontractor or agent, such as a design engineer, fall below the requisite standard. Of course, if the owner specifies and requires the use of a specific item, the owner may be giving an implied warranty that the specified item is suitable. If substitutions are to be permitted, the design professional or other appropriate party should investigate the proposed substitution and be able to demonstrate that the substitution is appropriate and will meet requirements.

48. Use Insurance To Help Manage Risk.

Insurance can be used to manage risk. If, for example, a partially completed structure collapses due to faulty design, the design professional would be liable for the resulting damages. Various insurance coverages may be available to cover certain of these damages. Generally, insurance provisions remain a mystery to procurement specialists.

Personal Injury And Property Damage

A professional's general liability ("CGL") policy would cover personal injuries and property damage to third parties.

Replacement of Non-Faulty Work
And Consequential Damages

The professional liability policy would cover the cost of damage to or replacement of non-faulty work. It would also cover consequential damages such as lost profits or expenses incurred as a result of faulty design or some other form of professional negligence.

Risk Of Faulty Work

The cost of removing, redesigning, or rebuilding the faulty work might not be covered by insurance. Check with your insurance specialist. However, the professional and the firm would be personally liable for the faulty work itself as part of the business risk subject to whatever limitations of liability the contract may contain. Also bear in mind that if a person or firm has no real assets (is "judgment proof"), you won't collect. As the saying goes, "You can't get blood from a stone."

Cost And Availability

Professional liability insurance can be expensive and may not always be available to all contractors. Even where available, coverages may have relatively low policy limits. The amount and extent of insurance is essentially a business decision which depends, in part, on how much risk the Company is willing to take. Bear in mind that insurance can reduce risk, but cannot make a transaction completely risk-free.

49. Consult With Your Insurance Specialist.

Your insurance specialist can advise you as to the cost and availability of coverage, as well as spot potential risks. For example, if a single policy is covering many different projects and insureds, all sharing the same coverage limits, there may not be enough insurance to cover all claims. Knowing who else is on the policy can help assess this risk. In certain situations, your insurance specialist may want to examine certified copies of insurance policies. He or she can also explain to you the difference between insurable risks and uninsurable ("pure" or business risks).

50. Avoid Being Named As An Additional Insured
    On A Professional Malpractice Policy.

Since owners are not providing professional services, they need not (and should not) be named as additional insureds under a professional malpractice policy, since the purpose of such a policy is to protect the owner against the consequences of professional negligence by the professional. If an owner is named as an additional insured under such a policy, it could mistakenly be named in a lawsuit alleging malpractice.

51. Ask Your Insurance Specialist To Help You
    Distinguish Between "Practice" and "Project"
    Policies.

Practice policies provide professional liability insurance to a firm and all the professionals working as employees of the firm. Larger projects can be separately insured under a "Project" policy. Typically, a project policy is issued in the name of the prime design firm with other design professionals working as subcontractors named as additional insureds.

One advantage of a project policy is that it provides coverage limits that cannot be diluted by claims arising out of other unrelated projects. Once a project is completed, a reporting period goes into effect, the length of which can vary. Generally, an extended reporting period is preferable.

52. Avoid Restricting Your Insurance and Indemnification Rights.

Contractual provisions limiting liability should not apply to or otherwise restrict insurance provisions protecting the owner, or to the contractual duty to defend, indemnify, and hold harmless the purchaser against infringement and personal injury claims or suits by third parties, particularly on large or dangerous projects.

53. Tailor The Contract To The Project.

Take time to carefully tailor the contract to the particular project. Tailoring the contract means more than simply using a "cut and paste" approach. It means a clear and complete articulation of each parties' rights and responsibilities. Contract documents which are incomplete, inconsistent, or inapplicable to the task can create problems. Also, be wary of standard form contracts prepared by trade associations representing architects, contractors, or engineers. These contracts usually do a good job of contractually protecting their respective "client" groups, but they may not meet your needs. Generally, you are much better off "controlling the paper" and developing your own contract rather than using someone else's document.

54. Take The Time To Plan And Reflect That Planning In The Written Contract.

206

Part of managing the risks associated with a project involves identifying and analyzing the risks involved. How likely are delays, changed conditions, or unusual events, and how could they affect the task? What if the deliverables do not live up to your expectations? Whose opinion or judgment will govern? Once those risks have been determined, the contract should reflect how the risks will be allocated, either by sharing or shifting the risks.

55. Determine The Roles To Be Played.

A certain supplier such as an engineer, architect, or construction manager can have more than one role on any particular project. He or she can have the status of a contractor or function as the purchaser's agent or even as an arbiter of disputes between the owner, contractor, and subcontractors.

56. Avoid Waiving "Time Of The Essence".

Some contracts may specify that "time is of the essence" which essentially means that you must have performance of the deliverables on the date specified, and if delivery is not made on time, there is no obligation on your part. If time of performance is to be made "of the essence", make sure the supplier understands your needs and that time of delivery is critical. Remember that if you continue to urge performance after the time set has passed, you may be waiving your right to time of the essence, i.e., the option to walk away from the deal. Make sure that your contract grants you the right to make new dates of the essence if the original dates are not met and you still want or need the deliverables. Be aware that interpretation of time of the essence provisions may vary depending on the particular jurisdiction or industry.

57. Avoid Inadvertent "Approvals".

Make it clear that any review of any work or deliverables by the owner is solely for the purpose of determining general consistency with overall project objectives and does not relieve the professional of responsibility for accuracy, completeness, and conformity with contract requirements. Likewise, any general superintendence exercised by the purchaser to ensure contract compliance should not relieve the supplier of its responsibilities.

58. Keep The Lines of Command Clear
    By Respecting "Privity of Contract".

The general rule is that only those who are parties to a contract (in "privity") have contractual rights and liabilities to each other. Developments in the law pertaining to UCC warranties and products liability actions have eroded this rule by permitting third parties such as family members or consumers to sue manufacturers and others for non-conforming or defective products. In addition, intended third party beneficiaries to a contract can also sue under the contract. For this reason, contracts should specify that there are no third party beneficiaries to the contract.

59. Watch Out For The "Multi-Prime" Trap.

If more than one firm is required on a project, it may be tempting for the owner to hire several firms. Because these suppliers are not in privity of contract with each other, they have no contractual obligations to each other. In addition, the purchaser is faced with managing and coordinating their individual efforts toward the collective goal in the face of what may be competing interests. Moreover, if the purchaser does all the hiring, it may be on the hook for actual or alleged mistakes made by those under contract with the owner. Therefore, many owners insist on "single-point" accountability by requiring that one firm hire all the professionals and others needed to accomplish the task. Some suppliers object to this because of the increased potential for liability due to errors and associated insurance premiums which may be based on a percentage of billings. However, the "prime" contractor can protect itself against these risks by indemnification and by being named as an additional insured on the subcontractor's liability policies.

60. Secure Good Termination Rights.

The highly personal and subjective nature of services makes it necessary to be able to end the relationship if performance is not satisfactory or where the purchaser loses confidence in the supplier of the services. The right to terminate the contract for either cause of convenience is an important protection for the purchaser. Since services may have nuances that are not completely reflected in the documents, some post-termination work may be required by the original author. The agreement should provide that any post-termination closeout services should be provided at contract prices. Also specify the return or turnover of all information and work in progress in the event of termination.

61. Promote Competition.

Typically, a very high percentage of service contracts are "sole" or "single" sourced. This suggests that competition and other market forces may not be being brought to bear on pricing or other commercial terms to the Company's full advantage. Even if you have narrowed your supplier base to a few key entities to capture economies of scale or other advantages, keep it a "horse race".

62. Watch Out When Hiring A Potential Competitor.

Preserving the confidentiality of and control over valuable information is especially important when doing business with a firm which could eventually become a potential competitor. Intellectual property can be protected by copyright or patent. In a changing world, this may not be seen as far-fetched as it may seem. Contractual agreements can be used to restrict disclosure or use of information such as trade secrets which is confidential and offers a competitive advantage.

63. Contract In Haste, Repent At Leisure.

The terms "partnering" and "strategic alliance" have been used to describe the relationship of the parties to a contract. These terms are of recent origin and are somewhat subjective. What the individual parties understand these terms to mean can differ substantially. As in any contractual undertaking, clearly and completely spell out your respective responsibilities and limit your liability as appropriate. If you are seeking a long-term relationship based on closer cooperation, make sure the prospective parties are compatible.

Depending on how it is defined in the agreement, a strategic alliance can mean forming an entirely new legal entity such as a partnership, joint venture, or corporation. Given the potential liability issues, tax consequences, and even antitrust implications, this requires careful planning and consideration at the highest levels of the corporation. However, a "strategic alliance" can also be nothing more than assuring a certain level of orders necessary to achieve economies of scale.

64. Identify The Success Factors.

A key step in planning a large-scale project or complex undertaking of any sort is to identify and prioritize the critical factors by which the success or failure of the project will be judged. The "mission" or objectives sought to be achieved should be clearly articulated, both internally and to the contractor with predetermined standards of performance. Note that the "success factors" and their relative importance may differ, depending on one's perspective. Total Quality Management ("TQM") can play a role in identifying the salient success factors.

65. Front-Load The Effort.

The old saying that "prevention is the best cure" is true in medicine and contracts. Spend enough time and effort on preparing a clear and complete document with a carefully written scope of work. The "cut and paste" method of preparing contracts can be dangerous. Avoid using outdated or inapplicable documents. It might be better to go to the expense of creating a well-crafted contract and avoid the cost of a failed project and subsequent "root cause" post mortem analysis. Poor scope documents can also drive costly changes and delays.

66. Know The Rules of Contract Interpretation.

How ambiguities are construed depends on whether the ambiguities were obvious, or should have been, to the reader. A supplier usually has a duty to inquire about any ambiguities in the contract documents, particularly where the ambiguity is obvious. Contracts can also reduce ambiguity by including an "order-of-precedence" clause identifying which documents govern in terms of priority.

67. Use The Contract As A Management Tool.

Contract management is the art of accomplishing a stated objective on time and within budget. Each procurement effort is unique and temporary effort. Although technical expertise is essential, good administrative and communication skills are also important. So is a good contract and a basic understanding of legal principles.

Preparing a contract tailored to the uniqueness of the project and which is clear and complete is a key "foundation". The contract's scope of work represents your detailed articulation of the project goals and objectives. The contract's performance standards represent what you deem to be the project's measure of success. The contract's administrative and control mechanisms provide the key tools in managing costs and schedule. Starting out with a good contract improves the odds of success.

68. Avoid The "Apparent Authority" Trap.

An employee or an agent is only allowed to act within the scope of authority as given by the principal, i.e., his or her employer. This authority can be either "actual" or "apparent". An employee or agent cannot, by his or her actions or statements, create authority which the principal has not given. However, an employer can inadvertently "cloak" someone with apparent authority which can have the same effect as giving an employee actual authority.

Actual authority consists of authority which is given in spoken or written form, i.e. "express", and includes any "implied" authority which would logically and reasonably be expected to accompany an employer's expressly stated authority. Apparent authority is also created by the principal. However, unlike actual authority which is given to the agent by the principal, apparent authority is created by how the principal acts toward third parties who reasonably rely on the principal's behavior.

69. Structure The Deal To Your Liking.

How you structure the deal is part of managing or allocating risks under the agreement. Contracts can be structured in any number of ways, including as:

<u>Lump Sum</u> – all stipulated work is provided in exchange for a fixed sum.

<u>Unit Price</u> – supplier is paid at a set per unit price based on total units.

<u>Cost Plus</u> – supplier is reimbursed for the cost of the work plus a specified fee.

<u>T&M</u> – supplier is paid for time and expenses such as materials or consumables.

<u>GMP</u> – supplier is reimbursed for the cost of the work plus a fee up to a set amount with possible shared savings below that amount.

<u>Target Price</u> – The parties agree on a well-documented estimated cost as the target price to be paid with shared risk for cost which exceed or under-run the target price.

The method of compensation will have a big impact on many of the contract clauses. For example, where costs are being reimbursed, clearly defining "costs" and specifying those costs which are reimbursable may be in order along with strong audit provisions. In a lump sum contract, the issue of what constitutes changes or extras looms large. Of course, different components of the contract can have different modes of compensation.

70. Lock In Price Protection
    And "Most Favored" Client Status.

You can agree that unless otherwise specifically provided herein, the price(s) stated in the contract are not subject to increase and that such price(s) and all other terms and conditions contained therein are not less favorable than those extended to any other customers for the same or similar work.

71. Be Familiar With General Damage Principles.

The law follows a "make whole" approach to contractual breaches. The non-breaching party is entitled to be compensated for "damages" - typically financial loss - resulting from the breach. These "compensatory" damages can be either direct or indirect. Direct damages are those directly attributable to the breach. By contrast, lost profits as a consequence of the breach would be an example of indirect or "consequential" damages.

Punitive damages are punitive rather than compensatory in nature. The purpose of punitive damages is to punish the wrongdoer. Such damages are not available for mere breach of contract but instead require some sort of intentional misconduct typically involving tortious, outrageous, or fraudulent behavior.

Note that there may not be any damages in the event of a breach. The cost of the same deliverables purchased elsewhere may be less than the original price, and, likewise, there may not be any consequential damages. In such a case, the non-breaching party would only be entitled to nominal (e.g. $1) damages.

The law follows the same "make whole" philosophy in cases where the default consists of a breach of warranty. In such cases the non-breaching party's damages are the difference in the value between the deliverables as provided compared to the value of the deliverables as warranted. If the damages would be difficult to determine, the parties can stipulate in advance on a reasonable forecast of the damages which would probably be incurred in the event of a breach.

72. Seek Compensation, Not Punishment.

Although penalty provisions in a contract are not enforceable, the parties can agree on the amount of damages which would occur in the event of a breach. Where actual damages would be difficult or impossible to calculate and the amount agreed to is a reasonable forecast of the damages which would be suffered, the parties can specify liquidated damages.

Care needs to be taken in setting the amount of liquidated damages. If set too high, such damages could be construed as an unenforceable penalty. If set too low, they could become an attractive option not to perform. Note that in cases where both parties are at fault, liquidated damages are not apportioned. In such cases the law reverts to traditional damage remedies with some jurisdictions using the stipulated sum as a "cap" on total recoverable damages.

In order to reduce the risk that the liquidated damages provisions are challenged as a penalty, the agreement should specify that: "The parties agree that in the event of [the Contractor's breach, failure to adhere to schedule, etc. . .] the harm to the Company would be very difficult to determine and that the amount of [ ] per day fixed as liquidated damages is not a penalty, but a reasonable forecast of just compensation for said harm." Consult with counsel.

73. Watch Out For "Hybrid" Contracts
    Involving Both Goods And Services.

The law starts you out with different rights and obligations, depending on whether the UCC or the common law applies. Of course, the law also allows tremendous "freedom of contract" to strike just about any deal you want provided it is not illegal or dishonest.

While the common law applies to services and the UCC applies to goods, most transactions involve a mixture of both. In such hybrid situations, the applicable law is determined by whether the sale of goods or the sale of services predominates.

74. Avoid Waiving Your Rights.

How the parties act or have acted in the past can be used to interpret what the contract really means. Avoid acting in a manner that is inconsistent with the contract. In addition, if a party reasonably relies on your conduct or statements to the parties' detriment, you could be precluded ("estopped") from asserting your rights. For example, if time is of the essence and you urge performance after that time has passed, you may lose your right to terminate for failure to meet the original time of the essence date.

75. Think Rights, Remedies, and Responsibilities.

The law accords commercial enterprises and businesspeople very broad discretion in contractually allocating risks and limiting liability. Develop a clear concept of what the respective parties' rights, remedies, and responsibilities will be and make sure they are reflected in the contract. Bear in mind that the traditional remedies of repair, replacement, or reperformance may not suit your needs. If something cannot be made to work or your needs change, you may wish to be able to seek a refund, damages, to terminate, or even injunctive relief.

76. Use Your Collective Corporate Experience.

Past experience, both in terms of what has worked or not worked well in other contracts, can help repeat earlier success and avoid past failures. Make sure that you use the entire "corporate" collective experience by keeping a list of "lessons learned" on past projects. Communicate. Electronic mail makes it easy to put everyone on "notice".

77. Seek Appropriate Assistance.

The "marketplace" is becoming increasingly sophisticated and complex. Use counsel and other specialists in helping to manage risk by contract.

78. Avoid the "Automatic Renewal" Trap

Contracts which "automatically" renew themselves are booby traps for the unwary. Such "evergreen" clauses where the purchaser is "kicked" into a renewal term for services (e.g., equipment or software leases or maintenance agreements) can have tragic and expensive consequences. Do not agree to such clauses, or at least require prior written notice that the initial term is about to expire.

79. Protect The Integrity Of The Process.

Promote and maintain the integrity of the competitive bidding process and other procurement efforts. Information concerning a vendor's bid should not be divulged to a competitor where the information is confidential or where disclosure would place the vendor at a competitive disadvantage. Likewise, confidential information about the Company's plans, preliminary decisions, or information which could place the Company at a disadvantage or give one bidder an advantage over another bidder should not be disclosed.

Also bear in mind that it is important that suppliers believe in the integrity of your process. Perception can be reality. Avoid even the appearance of impropriety and be familiar with the Company's Standards of Integrity.

80. Link Procurement to Planning

Time is the enemy of all good contracts. Negotiation, selection and contract preparation all take time. "Hurry-up" deals made in haste are usually a disaster. Linking procurement to the planning and budgeting process can give the procurement professional the time to do the job right.

81. Require Written Notice of Breach

If a supplier believes that the Company is guilty of any breach of its duties or obligations, it should not wait until the end of the contract to assert those claims. Requiring prompt written notice of any acts or omissions by the Company which the supplier believes were improper allows the Company to investigate the matter while the "trail is fresh" and to take steps to protect its interests. It also prevents any after-the-fact "sandbagging" if the project runs into difficulty. By the same token, the Company may wish to provide written notice of any breaches by the vendor. Such notice is an absolute requirement in UCC transactions.

82. Write Letters, Answer Correspondence and Document All Important Conversations

Following up telephone or other important conversations with a letter memorializes the discussion and creates a "record" which can be relied upon in the future after memories may have faded. In addition, failing to answer a letter or accusation may make it seem like you cannot contest the facts or that you agree with the positions taken. Such "tacit admissions" can come back to haunt you.

83. Be Specific About Your Training Needs.

If the deliverables include training, specify the number of employees to be trained, when, and where the training will take place, the duration of the training, and whether it will be continuous or segmented, the nature and number of the training materials and manuals, the qualifications of the individual(s) doing the training, and how travel or other expenses will be handled. Consider how replacement employees will be trained and whether the training could be videotaped.

84. Be Specific about Any Site Requirements.

If the buyer needs to perform any site preparation work, make sure the seller agrees that the deliverables will be compatible with the prepared site in terms of power needs, clearances, access, or environmental (temperature, humidity) needs or considerations.

85. Watch Out for the "Incorporation By Reference Trap"

Contract law says that you can "incorporate" or add documents to the contract and make them part of the deal simply by agreeing that "a document is part of the contract and is hereby incorporated by reference . . ." or words to the effect. Make sure you have a copy, read, and understand all "parts" of documents that make up the contract.

86. Preserve Your Negotiating Power

The quickest way to dilute your negotiating power and leverage is to enter into a contract on a piece-meal basis. That is why ill drafted letters of intent or other forms of preliminary agreements (e.g., memorandums of understanding) can be so dangerous. Seek counsel on how to word such documents or simply make it clear that there is "no deal" unless and until a written contract is formally executed or a purchase order is issued by the Company if that is what you intend.

87. Get It In Writing.

Don't make oral contracts or if you do, assume that they will be enforceable against you, but not in your favor.

88. Don't Fight The Battle Of The Forms.

The only sure way to "win" the battle of the forms is not to fight it. Get a signed contract for all high-risk deals.

89. Read And Understand What You Sign.

Don't sign what you have not read or what you do not understand.

90. Set The Risk For Loss In Transit

Specify who will be at risk for loss, damage, or destruction of goods in transit - the so-called delivery terms. Just as importantly, even if the supplier bears that risk, how quickly must the goods be repaired or replaced?

91. Fix The Point Of Acceptance.

Specify what constitutes acceptance of the deliverables - whether goods, services, or both. At a minimum, the deliverables should be deemed accepted only after a reasonable opportunity to inspect to insure that they conform to the contract requirements and satisfying any acceptance tests or "trial-use" periods specified.

92. Control The Moment Of Agreement.

Prior to making a contractual commitment, you retain all your options and negotiating power. After agreement, you lose your "walk-away" power, and any additional "negotiation" becomes much more difficult.

93. Preserve Your Leverage.

Tying payment to performance, progress, or milestones preserves your control over the process. Retain a portion of the purchase price until satisfactory completion and acceptance.

94. Protect Information.

Confidential or proprietary information is often exchanged in the course of negotiations or contract administration. This information has both competitive and commercial value. Use appropriate confidentiality and non-disclosure agreements and contract terms.

95. Plan for the Inevitable Disengagement

All good things come to an end. Think of the end at the beginning. Termination clauses and options allow you to disengage on your terms. Particularly in information technology or outsourcing contracts, plan for the "migration back" of all or part of the services either to another vendor or back to the Company.

REVIEW OF CONTRACTING STEPS AND PROCEDURES

It's always good to periodically review your contracting steps and procedures. The following list can be helpful in this regard:

1. Is the selection process careful and considered?

   a) Were several proposals solicited?
   b) Were the suppliers' records and capabilities evaluated?

2. Is the selected supplier solvent and adequately financed?

   a) Will subcontractors/suppliers be paid?
   b) Will remedies or monetary recovery be available?

3. Are the respective rights and responsibilities clearly stated?

   a) What will be delivered?
   b) What must be done and by whom?

4. How will payment be made?

   a) Is the price fixed or capped?

    b) Will payment be tied to performance?

5. How will change(s) be accommodated?

    a) Increases or decreases in price/costs
    b) Adding to or deleting from the deliverables

6. What are the risks associated with the transaction?

    a) What are the probabilities and consequences?
    b) How does the agreement allocate those risks?

7. Are the warranties and remedies adequate?

    a) Is "repair or replace" sufficient?
    b) What about "access" or "corrective action"?

8. Does the contract reflect the entire agreement?

    a) What isn't in the contract that should be?
    b) Are all the key representations reflected in the contract?

9. Is liability limited or capped in any way?

    a) Is a lot being risked to gain a little?
    b) Are rights or remedies unduly limited?

10. How will termination be handled?

    a) Are termination costs set forth?
    b) Is there a "disengagement" plan?

11. How will the contract be managed?

    a) Who will administer the contract?
    b) Who must know the contract's terms?

12. What is/will be the parties' relationship?

    a) Is it a one-time deal?
    b) Is it a long-term relationship?

13. What are the notice provisions?

    a) Is notice of breach required?
    b) What documentation will be provided?

14. What are the choice of law/venue provisions?

    a) What law will apply?
    b) Where will disputes be litigated?

15. Is intellectual property or confidential information involved?

16. What is the contract term and what are the renewal provisions?

THE CONTRACT MANAGEMENT PROCESS

All good contract management begins with good "self-management". The organization that seeks to have an effective contract management process needs to look at individual transactions to ensure that the procedures in place are both applicable and effective. For significant transactions a Contract Management Plan ("CMP") should be implemented which reflects not only the larger process but the individual contractual nuances.

1. The objective of a good contract management process is to achieve a well-defined, well-documented, easily understood process with consistently applied procedures and clearly-defined responsibilities that is designed to ensure that contractual objectives are met. It involves monitoring, measuring and managing contractual performance, costs and changes.

2. Although contract management is often focused on performance once the contract has been entered into, its degree of success is affected by:

    1. The quality of the "cradle-to-grave" process; including supplier selection and how well the parties have articulated their respective rights and responsibilities under the agreement,

2. The quality of project management; including tying payment to performance and ensuring that conforming deliverables are provided on time at the agreed upon price, and

3. The quality of contract administration; including whether invoices are paid on time, without over or duplicate payment, based on proper documentation.

4. The quality of the document control capability of the parties including the creation of contract documents as well as their storage and retrieval.

5. The quality of the resources the parties place on sound contract management including the proper training and staffing for the contract management process.

3. The contract elements to be managed include:

1) Performance	2) Costs	3) Changes
• Service Levels	• Prices	• Receipt
• Metrics	• Margins	• Recording
• Audit	• Trends	• Evaluation
• Escalation	• Unit Costs	• Implementation
• Disputes	• Asset Use	• Documentation
• Improvement	• Resource Use	• Communication
• Reports	• Discounts	• Migration

4. Contract management objectives include:

1) Ensuring compliance.
2) Monitoring costs and payments.

3) Documenting and applying lessons learned.
4) Measuring performance and service levels.
5) Maintaining performance history data bases.
6) Managing long-term contract relationships.
7) Managing increases or decreases to the scope of work.

5. Benefits of proper contract management include:

   1) Lessons are learned and mistakes are not repeated.
   2) Mistakes are avoided, minimized, or corrected early.
   3) Payment is made on time and correctly, without overpayment.
   4) Payment is tied to performance which is monitored/measured.

6. Essentially, contract management is the process of:

   1) Using knowledge and leverage to obtain favorable terms,
   2) Monitoring whether the parties are adhering to their bargain, and
   3) Managing the relationship and changes to the contract.

7. Poor contract management has its genesis in:

   1) Over reliance on suppliers and their contract documents,
   2) Failure to manage all phases of the transaction, including delivery and closure, as a coordinated whole, as well as
   3) Lack of accountability for, and failure to learn from, mistakes and past experience.

8. Causes of poor contract management include:

1) Imposed terms and conditions.
2) Contract terms never communicated to users.
3) Lack of clearly defined deliverables or objectives.
4) Failure to monitor, measure and record performance.
5) Lack of knowledge as to respective rights and responsibilities.
6) Failure to understand contract rights and responsibilities.
7) Failure to distinguish between "resource" and "results" contracts.
8) Lack of accountability for ignoring or waiving contract rights.
9) Inconsistent or conflicting terms or agreements.
10) Failure to make full use of competition.

9. The symptoms of poor contract management include:

1) Excessive costs or change orders.
2) Lack of document creating ability.
3) Lack of appropriate measures and controls.
4) Lack of performance data and history.

10. Consequences of poor contract management include.

1) Suppliers are not properly managed.
2) Results and objectives are not achieved.
3) Responsibilities are not met or performed.
4) Higher prices and costs are paid or incurred.
5) Rights and remedies are not exercised or waived.
6) Mistakes are made, ignored/covered up, and repeated.

11. Contract management processes (after signing) include:

1) Identify budget allocations.
2) Confirm resource commitments.
3) Assemble contract documents.

4) Make and document changes/modifications.
5) Identify respective rights and responsibilities.
6) Identify deviations from rights and responsibilities.
7) Take corrective action and monitor compliance.
8) Assess issues and take the appropriate action.
9) Monitor, measure and report on performance.
10) Manage "extra sales" initiatives or "back door" negotiations.

12. Contract management sub processes include:

1) Review contract documents.
2) Check for signatures, insurance, bonding etc.
3) Identify most "restrictive" provisions.
4) Identify critical dates such as:

- Start and End Dates.
- Delivery and Inspection Dates.
- Progress and Milestone Dates.
- Renewal Notice Dates.
- Termination Notice Dates.
- Impact Notice Dates.
- Warranty Start/Expiration Dates.
- Acceptance/test Dates.
- Payment Dates.

5) Identify key payment terms:

- Price.
- Escalation caps.
- Volume discounts.
- Liquidated and other damages.

- Type of compensation:
  - GMP.
  - Lump Sum.
  - T&M.
  - Cost Plus.
  - Fee.
  - Other.

6) Identify key performance terms:

- Service levels.
- Quality standards.
- Resources vs. Results.

7) Identify key personnel:

- Supplier key personnel.
- Purchaser key personnel.

8) Identify respective rights:

- Supplier's Rights.
- Purchaser's Rights.

9) Identify respective responsibilities:

- Supplier's Rights.
- Purchaser's Rights.

10) Identify Special Circumstances/Considerations:

- Lease Transactions.

- Professional Services.
- Outsourcing Contracts.

Every CMP should answer a series of "In the event that…" For example, with regard to the potential for delay claims a good CMP could state:

In the event Contractor claims a delay in its ability to perform its responsibilities, such claim shall be dealt with and addressed by [DESIGNATED COMPANY EMPLOYEE OR AGENT] who shall promptly review the claim and respond in accordance with the Contract terms and conditions. All such claims shall be assigned a number and filed according date received, Contractor and topic. The date on which the claim was responded to together with all relevant and supporting documentation shall be kept in a well-organized and retrievable manner. Prior to responding to the claim, the [DESIGNATED COMPANY EMPLOYEE OR AGENT] shall review the Contract and investigate the facts asking, at a minimum, the following questions:

1. Did a delay actually occur?
2. What/who caused the delay?
3. Was the critical path affected?
4. How does the contract allocate risk of delay?
5. Were the notice requirements complied with?
6. Has supporting documentation been provided?
7. Could the delay have been avoided/mitigated?
8. Are the alleged damages correctly calculated?
9. Are the alleged damages barred by the contract?
10. Were subject matter experts and management kept apprised?
11. Were all important discussions and decisions documented?
12. Was a response provided in accordance with the Contract?

THE TEN BASIC RULES OF GOOD CONTRACT MANAGEMENT

As in all things following the rules will keep you on the right track. These rules are simple but for some reason routinely violated despite serious consequences.

1. Rule No. 1 - No contract - No work.

Without a signed contract, the parties are subject to high defense costs and potential compensatory and consequential damages in the event of any actual or alleged breach. Large commercially-wise and sophisticated entities do not perform work without a written contract. Standard form-type agreements are readily available. However, such agreements need to be tailored for the individual transaction in terms of the Scope of Work or Deliverables. Be sure only persons with actual authority sign the contract. Where the other party's contract is used, appropriate exceptions need to be taken.

2. Rule No. 2. Develop a written scope of work.

A contract includes both commercial T's and C's (Terms and Conditions) and a written scope of work. Do not enter into oral contracts or honor verbal requests for work. Procurement and contract professionals can easily put in place agreements with potential parties covering the T's and C's for any work.

3. <u>Rule No. 3 - Respect the chain of command</u>.

A party should only deal with the party with whom it has a signed contract. Employees should not take orders directly from other than their employer. Taking orders directly from third parties violates what lawyers call "privity of contract".

4. <u>Rule No. 4. Document important conversations or events</u>.

It is a good idea to document important conversations or events. However, bear in mind that these documents could be held to be "discoverable" - the other side gets to see them in the event of litigation. Be accurate and clear.

5. <u>Rule No. 5. Double-check all estimates</u>.

Assume nothing. Question everything, especially costs and assumptions.

6. <u>Rule No. 6. Have a single point of contact</u>.

Have a single point of contact between the parties. The more people get involved, the greater the risk of mistake and miscommunication.

7. <u>Rule No. 7. Get written authorization for changes</u>.

Never request or permit "extra" or out-of-scope work without written authorization.

8. Rule No. 8. Notify the other party of any breach or problems.

A party should promptly provide written notice to the other party of any breach, delay, change, or problem which was not anticipated by the contract.

9. Rule No. 9. Identify and evaluate the risks.

Identify and make a list of the risks and evaluate those risks in terms of their probability and consequences. Weigh the potential for success against the consequences of failure. Make a list of ways to manage and control the risks. Avoid risking a lot to gain a little or more than you can afford to lose. Manage and control the risk by structuring the transaction so as to maximize "high reward, low risk" potential.

10. Rule No. 10. Check with the professionals.

When in doubt, check with purchasing and contract professionals. They are trained to help you identify and allocate risk by contract, but they need the facts. Help them help you by getting the complete and accurate facts.

CONTRACTING PLAYBOOK

As noted, organizations are charged with creating lean, flexible and competitive business models focusing on:

a. Delivering sustainable cost improvement
b. Transforming business support capabilities
c. Integrating diverse procurement organizations
d. Accomplishing more, faster by working more efficiently

Delivering continuous improvements will require achieving world class performance commercial sophistication coupled with tools and skill sets. This includes a structured methodology for entering into commercial transactions fostering quality and consistency.

Essentially, management is being asked to do more with less. Nowhere is this more evident than in the area of human capital. There are multiple aspects to this problem including:

a. Fewer employees but more work
b. New employees with little experience
c. Experienced employees with legacy experience

Employees may have one year's experience 30 times. Moreover, training new employees is expensive and time consuming. Lack of consistency, coordination and application of lessons learned are likewise ongoing challenges. This begs the question "How do we get consistent and correct execution and results?" The solution is a standardized "Contracting Playbook" approach.

What is a Contracting Playbook? It is a standardized and collaborative step by step contracting process which articulates each step necessary to enter into well structured transactions.

The benefits of this approach are:

a. Leverages existing resources.
b. Allows less experienced professionals to stay on course.
c. Keeps experienced professionals from deviating from standards.
d. identifies potential areas for improvements including:

1. deleting duplicative / unnecessary steps.
2. highlighting potential gaps or weak points in the process.

Each step is linked to a set of documents such as templates, desktop procedures, forms and checklists to ensure that the associate has the necessary tools.

There are of course innumerable so-called "Contract Management Systems" on the market or which have been developed at huge expense with very little practical payout. In reality Contract management systems are often so impractical that they are under-utilized or end up as mere document repositories. Moreover, Contract management systems do not typically link the user with tools for contract formation, administration and close out. Finally, Typical contract management systems do not include a step by step process for entering into, managing the contracts from "cradle-to-grave".

How is a Contracting Playbook different? It provides a clear cradle-to-grave process and road map for creating sound commercial transaction as well as a centralized storage facilitating ease of retrieval and sound audit trail. It must be user friendly and accessible on a collaborative basis and provides a clear process for RFPs, scope development, proposal assessment, internal controls and risk management protocols, addressing claims and warranty issues and a complete well defined sequence from kick-off to closeout including the use of standardized forms, letters and templates.

What would the Contracting Playbook look like? The table below outlines the basic process and steps to be followed for entering into Contracts / Agreements and commercially managing these transactions from start to finish in an active and proactive manner in support of operational requirements.

CONTRACTING PLAYBOOK PROCESS AND PROCEDURES				
NO.	PROCESS (Steps)	DESCRIPTION (Inputs-Activities-Actions-Outputs)	RESPONSIBILITY (Governance)	LINK (Resource)
1				
2				
Etc.				

The steps listed are intended to be sequential recognizing that certain steps can be taken in parallel or made out of sequence as necessary. The advantages are clear. New and experienced employees utilize the step by step contract development and administration process flow with each step:

a. Organized and identified sequentially
b. Described (inputs, activities, actions, outputs)
c. Linked to the accountable party (buyer, client, stakeholder)
d. Linked to the appropriate tools, forms, desktops or templates

This results in a structured and organized process which reduces risk, improves efficiency, promotes consistency and fosters integration.

In conclusion the Contracting Playbook addresses every aspect of the total spend cycle, links tools with output in an integrated process, documents the process for assessing and identifying needs, suitable suppliers, sourcing strategies, risks, on-going performance and lessons learned and perhaps most importantly permits process improvement and workforce optimization. This approach can be used on either a project or transaction basis. The key is the upfront preparation with buy-in from all stakeholders.

IDENTIFYING "GAPS AND TRAPS" IN THE PROCESS

1. <u>**Maintain a "Big Picture / Long Term" Perspective.**</u>

   1) The transaction should allow purchaser to achieve its objectives at a cost and with the capabilities that allow the purchaser to be and stay competitive, including the right to make changes or terminate the arrangement and migrate to new technologies or suppliers. Plan for and build into the contract the flexibility to deal with continuous "whitewater".

   2) Transaction risks and options should be evaluated, e.g., what are the risks and costs of ownership vs. the risks and costs of leasing; performing work in-house vs. outsourcing, etc. and risk mitigation strategies put in place. Have a rigorous protocol for identifying and evaluating risk by both probability and consequences.

   3) The transaction and contract management process should be tailored to the particular situation. For example, in the context of software licenses, good contract management might mean developing and maintaining a current inventory of all software

licenses, avoiding purchasing software licenses or maintenance that is not needed, tracking software usage and restrictions to avoid legal liability, having ready access and reference to software license terms and conditions, and tracking total life-cycle costs, not just the initial purchase price.

2. **Avoid Seams In Accountability**

1) Undefined "hand-off" point where supplier'(s) accountability ends and the Buyer's begins (e.g., contractor vs. contractor, contractor vs. designer, contractor/designer vs. Buyer).

2) Lack of compatibility with adjoining systems, configurations, or components.

3) Use of "evergreen" automatic renewals instead of securing the option (but not the obligation) to renew, at an appropriate price.

4) Lack of list or "inventory" of all existing equipment or items to avoid overbuying or unnecessary commitments.

3. **Conflicts of Interests and Divided Loyalties**

1) Employees in a position to affect or influence procurement decisions with a familial or financial interest.

2) Suppliers in a position to affect or influence procurement decisions by recommending or promoting their approaches, solutions, designs, or selecting other suppliers.

4. **<u>Uncoordinated Or Designated Procurements</u>**

   1) Lack of coordination between various deals such as purchase/ lease of equipment/software and maintenance contracts.

   2) Failure to factor in total life-cycle costs (e.g., cost to maintain, upgrade, replace).

5. **<u>Poor Payment Practices</u>**

   1) Failure to structure "pay for performance" terms or take advantage of negotiated volume discounts reflected in the agreement.

   2) Failure to enforce clauses limiting price increase to stipulated increases upon proper prior notice.

   3) Failure to calculate and claim liquidated or other damages or exercise setoff or withholding rights.

6. **<u>Poor Tracking And Document Control</u>**

   1) Using supplier-prepared contract documents.

   2) Failure to have ready access to copies of contract documents.

   3) Failure to: specify and stay within scope, i.e., paying for work twice, ordering excessive "extra" work, properly track usage terms or restrictions (e.g., software licenses), make most effective use of contract rights and remedies (e.g., asserting warranty claims), manage legal liability.

7. **Identify The Control (Choke) Points**

    1) Controlling back-door extra sales initiatives.

    2) Maximizing negotiating power and leverage.

    3) Using the RFP Process to foster competition.

    4) Managing the points of agreement and acceptance.

    5) Setting and verifying test and acceptance procedures and criteria.

8. **Managing Contracts By Dates**

    1) Start/end dates
    2) Delivery date(s)
    3) Acceptance date(s)
       - Inspections
       - Test Protocol

    4) Milestone date(s)
       - Progress
       - Phased delivery

    5) Payment dates (tied to milestones?)

    6) Warranty Date(s)
       - Start
       - End
       - Extensions

7) Maintenance date(s)
   - Gaps?
   - Responsibility for?
   - Necessity of?
   - Termination?
   - Options?

8) Notice dates
   - Renewals
   - Termination
     •Cause
     •Convenience
   - Events
     •Changes
     •Delays
     •Force Majeure

9) Other key control dates.

TERMINATING CONTRACTS

The need to terminate a particular contract or transaction can be an enormous challenge for the supply chain management professional as well as others involved in the process. Having a step-by-step approach as articulated below is recommended.

1.0   Decide To Explore Termination Option(s)

    1.1   Termination for cause or convenience

    1.2   Full or partial termination

2.0   Understand Motivation To Explore Termination

    2.1   Breach of contract; and or,

    2.2   Dissatisfaction with performance; or,

    2.3   Changed or changing needs/requirements

3.0 Apprise Counsel And Subject Matter Experts

3.1 Advise counsel that termination is being explored

3.2 Coordinate investigation with counsel, if appropriate

3.2 Coordinate with subject matter experts, if appropriate

4.0 Conduct Investigation

4.1 Identify and review key contract clauses

4.2 Identify any termination costs/fees

4.3 Collect/develop facts and data

4.4 Assess potential damages, claims, counterclaims, back-charges, withholdings or setoffs

5.0 Evaluate Options And Risks

5.1 Consider alternatives

5.2 Assess and evaluate risks

5.3 Determine pros and cons

5.4 Identify "closeout" requirements

6.0   Decide On Course Of Action

6.1   Non-termination course [Alternatives]

6.2   Provide notice of breach and

6.3   Demand cure, repair, refund; and or,

6.4   Demand assurances; and or,

6.5   Other [See below]

7.0   Termination course

7.1   Cause

7.2   Convenience

8.0   Prepare Notice Of Termination

8.1   Seek legal review/input

8.2   Cite reason(s) and cite contract clause(s)

8.3   State effective date of termination

8.4   State "closeout" requirements/obligations

9.0   Retrieve Company Property/Information

9.1   Access/ID cards/authorization; and or,

9.2   Data, information, codes; and or,

9.3   Tangible items, e.g., keys, vehicles, facilities

10.0 Communicate Termination Decision

10.1 Provide personal communication; and or,

10.2 Provide written notice of breach. See step 8.0

11.0 Closeout Contract

11.1 Manage process; administer migration to new supplier/ solution; obtain releases if appropriate

11.2 Determine whether subcontractors have been paid

11.3 Inventory, inspect, acceptance, or reject portions of deliverables provided prior to termination and make final payment/billing as appropriate

DISPUTE RESOLUTION

It's best to think about dispute resolution early on in the process and incorporate your method for dealing with disputes into the contract. Disputes are inevitable and there needs to be a predictable mechanism for dealing with those disputes. The dispute resolution process is different than the process for dealing with claims for extra compensation, alleged delays, claims of force majeure or the like.

Typically all claims will have a process which needs to be followed which includes notice of the claim within certain specific time lines followed by adequate documentation supporting the claim factually. However, if the dispute or difference of opinion cannot be amicably resolved what is the path forward? Some contracts provide for an escalation procedure within the parties' respective organization but this doesn't guarantee an agreement will be reached. Escalation procedures are fine provided they have strict time frames and don't preclude either party from eventually getting to court or arbitration.

In addition, be leary of kicking all decisions upstairs to top or senior executives who may not know or have the time to know all the facts, background or circumstances. Some agreements provide that disputes will be mediated by an independent third party but mediation typically does not result in a binding commitment or obligation. And, unless you used a court appointed mediator you could end up having to pay a lot of money and spend considerable time in connection with mediation. Mediators will want to be paid and you'll spend time away from work preparing for and in the mediation process. As noted, mediation won't definitively give you a resolution since mediators are basically just trying to get both parties to voluntarily agree. This leaves two basic mechanisms for contract dispute resolution: litigation or arbitration.

Litigation involves a judge and jury with well-defined rules of discovery. Resort to the court system is essentially using the offices of a branch of government (the judiciary) either federal or state as appropriate. Judges are either appointed or elected depending upon the jurisdiction and you always have the right to appeal if you believe the court below made any factual or legal errors.

Arbitration involves not a court or a judge but either an arbitrator or panel of arbitrators. Arbitrators are private citizens who may have some expertise in a particular field but are not necessarily lawyers. There is a notion that arbitration is faster and cheaper than litigation but this is not necessarily the case. You don't pay for a judge or jury except for relatively minor filing fees.

If you hire an arbitrator(s) you will pay not only for the arbiter but the facilities in which the arbitration takes place as well as fees to the organization (e.g. the American Arbitration Association) for administering the arbitration. These can add up very quickly especially if your arbitration takes place where you are picking up the tab for the arbitrators hotel or other travel expenses. And, even if you specify a certain venue in your contract (e.g. New York City), and your arbitrator "requests" that the hearings take place in another location (e.g. White Plains, NY), you're going to be hard pressed to say "No".

In addition, absent fraud, arbitrators are the sole judges of the facts and law. There is no appeal even in the face of a mistake in law or the facts absent some blatant conflict of interest or fraud. You are stuck with that decision, right or wrong. In addition, the practical reality is that although arbitration provides for discovery along the lines of what you get in court, the extent of discovery an arbitrator may choose to allow can be substantially less than you would otherwise be entitled to if you were in court. Moreover, some arbitrators may be swayed by very abstract notions of "fairness" which might not seem fair to you especially if you have done a good job on a tight contract with clear responsibilities for each party.

Also consider that once a court case starts the hearings tend to be continuous until completed. Not so with arbitration, which can sometimes meet intermittently over a period of weeks, or even months. Something can get lost in that kind of process where there isn't a seamless continuity. Of course arbitrators are just people and may not have the same level of "impartiality" as a judge who knows that their opinions are subject to review via appeal. In essence arbitrators are "judge, jury and hangman" all in one so to speak. It's also a lot easier to look up a judge's record of decisions and find out how a particular judge has looked at the same or similar cases. Because arbitration decisions are private and confidential, you may have no clue as to how the arbitrator may choose to look at a particular issue.

My personal opinion is that arbitration is a much more uncertain process as compared to litigation. That's because you generally know the judge you get in terms of how he or she has ruled before and you know that the appeal process guarantees that the judge will follow the law and applicable precedent. The public natures of a trial as opposed to the closed door arbitration sessions also in my view encourage witnesses to be honest and straight forward. I would be very careful about giving up the right to a jury trial since jury's tend to be possessed by a lot of common sense and a practical way of looking at things.

OUTSOURCING: AVOIDING THE HAZARDS AND PITFALLS

The following are some general contract management principles regarding outsourcing contracts. It is designed to bring a sense of some of the strategic concerns and generic contract management issues associated with outsourcing. Outsourcing contracts tend to be unique and "fact-sensitive". Specifics need to be addressed on an individual basis.

1. UNDERSTANDING THE DRIVERS

Intense competition is forcing corporations to simultaneously cut costs and improve quality. In response, organizations are increasingly focused on their core competencies and relative competitive strengths. In order to meet their competitive challenges, many corporations are outsourcing non-core functions to highly specialized firms who can bring their expertise and efficiencies to bear on the outsourced functions. Although outsourcing has its drawbacks and should not be viewed as a panacea, under the right circumstances, and with due sensitivity to the associated risks and potential pitfalls, outsourcing can be a part of overall "smart sourcing" and make good business sense.

The primary reason to outsource is not simply to reduce costs, but instead, to obtain resources and capabilities that will improve the ability to compete. Given that the stakes are high and the consequences so long-lasting, the decision to outsource needs to be carefully considered and based on well-documented data. In particular, both existing and targeted performance levels must be determined, and associated business and legal risks, together with the potential advantages and disadvantages, need to be evaluated. Functions identified as potential outsourcing opportunities also need to be well-understood. An attempt to reengineer or otherwise "fix" so-called "broken" internal functions should be made before outsourcing them. Most importantly, both existing baseline performance and future service levels (with the goal of continuous improvement) against which the external provider's performance can be judged must be established before any agreement is reached.

2. OUTSOURCING IS NOT NEW

Most corporations engage in some form of outsourcing and have for years. Manufacturers have long used "outsourcing" to obtain certain parts or components of the products they make. Many functions like food, maintenance, security, and a variety of administrative services are now routinely performed by external providers. In addition, there has been an increase in the outsourcing of functions which may be essential, but are not the essence of a corporation's comparative advantage. For example, complex and highly specialized IT functions are being outsourced. Aside from IT, other crucial but non-core business processes are also being outsourced. Even governmental entities are turning to outsourcing under the rubric of "privatization" as a means of dealing with budget limitations.

3. FAVORABLE PRESS REPORTS

It is a fact of life that corporations prefer to issue positive press releases. Sometimes "publicity" is part of the "bargain" made between the purchaser and the external provider. Moreover, most press reports are written during the initial or "honeymoon" phase of the outsourcing agreement when huge savings or other benefits are anticipated. Although there are some negative stories regarding the risks and potential pitfalls of outsourcing (and predicting an eventual "insourcing" response), most reported press has been positive. Some surveys even report a positive correlation between high levels of outsourcing and stock market performance.

4. BUSINESS PROCESS OUTSOURCING

Another reason for the outsourcing bandwagon is that virtually all the large consulting firms are pursuing outsourcing as a major business opportunity as part of the "commodization" of generic services. Essentially, larger consulting firms are advising their clients to consider not only IT outsourcing, but "Business Process Outsourcing" or "BPO" which can include some or all (the "Keys to the Kingdom" approach) non-core competencies.

5. COORDINATING AND MANAGING THE EFFORT

Outsourcing contracts are complex. One of the many challenges to overcome as consulting firms and IT providers move into the Business Process Outsourcing market will be for purchasers to manage and coordinate the effort, particularly where several external providers are expected to interact with each other while controlling multiple corporate functions. Corporations need to be prepared to spend money (say eight to ten percent of the value of the outsourcing agreement) and talent to manage the effort. Make sure the persons charged with managing the outsourcing contract have the necessary skill sets. Managing a department with the emphasis on coordinating the efforts of employees, is a lot different than managing an outsourcing contract.

6. THE RELATIONSHIP: SUPPLIER OR PARTNER?

The relationship between an external provider and the corporation should be structured as a close and long-term relationship based on continuous process improvement built upon clearly-defined expectations, goals, and metrics. Resist the temptation to place an "alliance" or "partnership" label on the relationship. This is because the considerations that go into choosing and contracting with a "partner", as opposed to a supplier, are complex.

In an outsourcing context, the term "partnering" or "strategic alliance" is usually intended to mean an attempt at replacing an "adversarial" approach with a sharing of the risks and rewards associated with achieving common objectives. The terms "partnering" or "strategic alliance" should not be used to describe an outsourcing agreement unless the contract is structured to reflect a true partnering relationship or strategic alliance, i.e. a close working relationship based on trust, communication, and mutual dependency where both parties have a vested interest in reducing costs and achieving a favorable business outcome. That means that the external provider's "reward" must be based on results or meeting objectives rather than simply being compensated to "try hard" or perform discreet tasks.

Most outsourcing deals should not be "partnerships" or "strategic alliances". Usually, a straight "supplier" relationship is all the parties need or want. Moreover, it can be very dangerous to refer to a relationship as a strategic alliance or partnership when, in fact, it is nothing more than a traditional contract. Typically, "partners" in a legal sense can act as each other's agent and owe one another "fiduciary" duties. That's not the type of relationship you want to have with everyone.

7. WHAT SHOULD BE OUTSOURCED?

Manufacturers of goods have long struggled with "make or buy" decisions and have continually explored how to source on a "cheaper, faster, better" basis.

Theoretically, anything and everything could be outsourced except for essential policy and strategy making mechanisms. Even if a careful "cost-benefit" analysis is made, the ultimate decision may well be a matter of judgment. The danger is that the decision to outsource could be made in an arbitrary, random and piecemeal basis rather than as part of a well-conceived business plan. The focus should not be simply to reduce costs, but rather to achieve corporate strategic objectives as part of an overall business plan.

Deciding what to outsource starts with deciding what core competencies provide the organization's comparative advantages. For example, a publisher could decide that the content is "core", but that printing and distribution are not. A bank might decide to outsource check processing, but not loan approvals. The federal government might outsource medical veterans care, but not commanding combat troops. However, defining and drawing a "bright line" as to what is or is not core may not always be easy. The tendency is to define what one does as core or critical and what everyone else does as non-core or less critical. Note that what seems to be "core" can change over time.

Instead of trying to decide the ultimate question, it makes sense to identify "high potentials" for selective outsourcing (out-tasking specific services) and prioritize the effort in those areas where the internal sources are delivering "high cost, low quality" goods or services. Non-core functions that are transaction oriented, repetitive processes (e.g., food, maintenance, security or administrative services) which are relatively simple and easily segregated from other corporate activities have traditionally been identified as high potentials for outsourcing.

The decision regarding what and when to outsource can also depend on the type of change-immediate and dramatic vs. gradual and incremental-which the corporation seeks to make. For example, outsourcing can be used to quickly reduce barriers to entry into a new market (the "concept to customer" scenario) by using external sources to provide specialized expertise and/or new technology.

8. STEPS FOR OUTSOURCING

Outsourcing should be a well-organized process that is based on accurate and comprehensive information. Essentially here's an outline of what needs to be done:

1. Develop a comprehensive business plan to achieve the corporation's objectives;

2. Decide what functions are the essence of a corporation's comparative advantage;

3. Understand the process to be outsourced, the performance metrics, and the objectives sought to be achieved.

4. Identify and evaluate non-core functions for potential outsourcing based on a careful cost benefit analysis;

5. Understand both the corporation's and the external provider's cost structures and profit margins;

6. Search for, identify, and extensively screen potential suppliers form existing and other sources.

7. Clearly and completely articulate the parties' respective responsibilities with well-defined process improvement requirements and performance metrics, while anticipating changes in needs and technology.

8. Develop a detailed contract with input from legal and business experts and avoid using the external provider's standard form of agreement;

9. Make a careful and considered selection as to which supplier can best perform the work and meet the corporation's objectives;

10. Develop a migration plan for transitioning the function(s) to the external provider(s);

11. Exercise continuous and active cost control, monitoring, process improvement, and oversight; and

12. Have in place a "transition back" plan that allows the corporation to "recapture" the function or permits it to "migrate" to a new supplier in the event disengagement becomes necessary.

It is also critically important to have a "communication plan" with employees about what is being done and to coordinate the effort with the corporation's Human Resources experts.

9. POTENTIAL ADVANTAGES TO OUTSOURCING

1. *IMPROVED SERVICE LEVELS*

An external provider with specialized expertise and access to the latest advances in technology and processes can deliver improved quality provided there is the incentive to stay focused on client needs and objectives.

2. *REDUCED COSTS*

The price of outsourced services should reflect economies of scale and increased efficiency, including dealing with demand variability. The sale of equipment or facilities previously used to perform the function can also be a source of funds.

3. *FEWER DISTRACTIONS*

Outsourcing functions previously performed internally frees management from the burden of daily control and allows it to focus on strategic initiatives.

4. *RESOURCE ALLOCATION*

Goods or services can be obtained on a "pay-as-you-go" basis without the need to make long-term capital investments. It can also provide resources on an "as needed" basis regardless of "peaks and valleys" in demand.

5. *PROCESS IMPROVEMENT*

Access to new technology, world-class processes, as well as faster delivery, are also potential advantages.

10. POTENTIAL RISKS IN OUTSOURCING

1. *LOSS OF CONTROL*

If management abdicates the entire process to the external provider and fails to continuously and actively manage the contract and relationship, loss of control and key skills can result in overdependency (the "hostage-on-a-pirate-ship" scenario). If the extreme provider does not make the right investments, technological obsolescence is a big risk. Ironically, outsourcing could also restrict the ability to engage in further restructuring if the contract cannot be changed, or there is no viable exit plan.

2. *LOSS OF CLIENT FOCUS*

The external provider's goals and objectives may differ from those of the client, and over time may lose touch with the corporation's business plan and strategy, particularly where change is frequent or significant.

3. *LACK OF CLARITY*

The failure to clearly articulate and agree upon the parties' respective responsibilities is a major concern which can lead to costly and disruptive disputes and claims of "extra" or so-called "out of scope" work.

4. *LACK OF COST CONTROL*

Changes in company objectives and escalating pricing can drive costs beyond expectations, particularly if the contract does not include long-term pricing with built-in incentives to stay competitive, control costs and improve quality.

5. *LOSS OF GOODWILL*

Possible adverse reaction by employees and resultant damage to workforce morale as well as loss of corporate identity are risks that need to be considered and managed.

11. UNDERSTANDING THE MARGIN

If not properly managed, outsourcing can lead to loss of control. The risk is that losing the ability to perform the work internally will lead to overdependency. In addition, barriers to entry, such as the time and expense necessary to train a workforce to become knowledgeable about the corporation's specialized needs and requirements may hamper the ability to shift to another external provider. If not properly managed, the original "savings" or "benefits" may disappear.

Unless the corporation has access to and understands the supplier's cost structure and ongoing cost reduction and control mechanisms are part of the contract, suppliers will be tempted to raise prices in order to increase their margins. Throughout the outsourcing relationship, costs will have to be discussed, negotiated and controlled as part of a continuous joint effort by both parties. Simply outsourcing a function may not actually reduce costs long-term unless it is recognized that every activity has costs regardless of who's performing them. The need for, and cost of, activities needs to be continually evaluated and maintained, reduced, or eliminated as appropriate.

12. FULL-SERVICE OR BEST-OF-BREED?

External providers typically fall into two basic categories: So-called "full-service" firms that can handle all aspects of one or more functions or "best-of-breed" firms that specialize in particular areas.

Using a single firm avoids the need to coordinate the efforts of multiple providers. However, using a number of specialized firms allows corporations to benefit from unique expertise. Either approach will require strong relationship and contract management skills on the part of the corporation.

13. FACILITIES MANAGEMENT

One form of outsourcing is to turn over the management of a particular facility to an external provider. The facility manager becomes responsible for the operation of the facility, including staffing and daily operation. This arrangement can be structured as either simply a management function or a formal transfer of the facility, including staff and equipment, to a facilities management company. In an outsourcing arrangement, the corporation's employees are typically transferred to an external provider and may be performing their work at a new site operated by their new employer. That is not always the case under a facilities management agreement

14. TRANSITIONAL OUTSOURCING

Outsourcing can take different forms with many possible variations on the theme. Traditional outsourcing contemplates what is essentially a permanent transfer of responsibilities to an external provider under long-term (5 to 10 years) contracts. By contrast, transitional outsourcing is a "project" based, relatively short term (1-3 years) effort. The objective is to provide a corporation with assistance in undertaking a new effort and training its employees to eventually take over the entire effort.

For example, in an IT context an external provider could be hired to build a new system, and over time train and transition the entire responsibility for operation and maintenance back to corporate employees. Although initially the effort will be heavily staffed by the external provider, the idea is that corporate employees will work alongside and eventually take over the responsibility. This approach avoids situations where new systems or software are delivered and turned over with insufficient training and in-house expertise. In-house expertise and independence is retained with the benefit of external experience and expertise.

Whether a single "full-service" or several "best-of-breed" firms are used, it is important to remember that expertise resides in individuals and that "full-service" firms may not have the best talent in all areas. Even large external providers often "partner" or subcontract with other providers in an effort to deliver a "seamless global solution" to a client's business strategy and goals.

15. THE SELECTION PROCESS: USING RFPs OR RFIs

Requests for proposals ("RFPs") and Requests For Information ("RFIs") can be a powerful part of any procurement process, including making a careful selection of which external provider(s) to use. RFPs and RFIs can be especially useful as a means to gain knowledge and identify a "short-list" of promising candidates. In addition, a good proposal can be the basis of the work scope portion of the contract. Given the importance that compatibility and a close working relationship will play in the success of the outsourcing effort, a framework for extensive personal assessment makes sense. The following five steps are one approach:

1. *DUE DILIGENCE*

Part of making a careful selection is doing the background research regarding the candidates' references and capabilities. Financial strength, capabilities, reputation, and past experience need to be verified and documented.

2. *BRAINSTORMING*

Inviting candidates to bring three or four key personnel to spend a day or so brainstorming potential approaches and solutions with the client's employees is a good way to get a sense of problem solving, communication, and teamwork skills (and getting free consulting advice).

3. *PROVIDER PRESENTATIONS*

Giving candidates the opportunity to deliver a presentation can be a further test of their organizational, problem solving, communications, and interaction skills. By specifying that certain aspects of the proposal be addressed in greater detail, additional information can be obtained.

4. *STRUCTURED EVALUATIONS*

Creating a formal mechanism by which to objectively grade the candidate's proposals, presentations, and capabilities can help reduce bias or subjectivity. Factors such as costs, expertise, risks, and advantages can be weighed, depending on how the corporation views those factors.

5. *EXECUTIVE INTERVIEWS*

Having the final one or two contender(s) interviewed by the corporation's top officer(s) provides senior executive input and buy-in for the fateful decision. It is also a final check to ensure compatibility and a strategic fit with the corporation's goals and objectives.

16. ARTICULATING RESPECTIVE RESPONSIBILITIES

Regardless of whether the parties are considering forming a so-called "strategic alliance" or entering into a traditional "buyer-supplier" relationship, clearly and completely articulating the parties' respective responsibilities is by far the most important part of any outsourcing arrangement.

1. *AVOID "HANDSHAKE" DEALS.*

It would be the gravest of errors to assume that simply because the parties are contemplating some form of "partnering" or otherwise becoming "strategically allied" (with all its potential variations and differing connotations) that a detailed and specific written agreement is not necessary.

2. WHY YOU NEED A SCOPE DOCUMENT.

Clearly defining the parties' respective responsibilities is crucial for several important reasons. First, it is the basis on which the provider will set its pricing. Second, it is the basis on which the purchaser will make its selection. Finally, a clear understanding of the parties' respective responsibilities will protect against the risk of surprise and differing expectations. This is especially important so as to avoid subsequent disputes over claims for "extra" or "out-of-scope" work. Moreover, a well-defined work scope with clearly-defined performance metrics will permit performance to be monitored and measured.

3. USE RESPONSES TO THE RFP AS A STARTING POINT.

Once the parties have decided on their respective responsibilities, the services and other deliverables to be provided should be articulated into a work scope. This work scope can be either a separate document to be incorporated into the contract by reference or be included in the body of the contract. Often, written proposals received in response to the purchaser's Request For Proposal ("RFP") can be the starting point for creating the work scope. The work scope should clearly define what the external provider is expected to accomplish with specified service levels and performance standards. Turnaround time, milestones, performance schedules, and acceptance testing or criteria should also be addressed as appropriate. As previously indicated, a well-drafted work scope can help avoid disappointments based on differing expectations and minimize costly changes, delays, and disputes.

17. PAYING FOR VALUE AND PERFORMANCE

Given the importance of achieving the corporation's strategic goals and objectives, saving money shouldn't be the only or even the predominant reason to outsource. The focus should be on paying for value, not just saving money. Ideally, the "price" to be paid should reflect "value" received. Measuring value based on shared risks and rewards can be very difficult. Clearly specifying the "metrics" both hard (e.g., number of tasks successfully performed) and soft (e.g., client feedback surveys) is crucial.

Essentially, the objective is to pay for performance based on specified service levels with built-in incentives to share the benefits of reduced costs while maintaining the initial momentum to reduce cost. The idea is to deliver a "favorable business outcome".

New software tools are available that can help corporations manage outsourcing by tracking costs, performance, and quality criteria. The software can model the external provider's cost structure, thereby helping the corporation to understand the provider's margin.

18. DURATION AND RENEWALS

External providers will usually prefer relatively long-term (five to ten years) agreements whereas purchasers will typically want a shorter term (three to five years). The trend seems to be toward shorter-term agreements in order to provide the external provider with a continued incentive to perform and facilitate "exit" strategies.

Unlike other types of transactions, an outsourcing contract can never be allowed to simply expire. The whole point of an outsourcing arrangement is continuity of service. Moreover, it may take a year or more to select and transition to an alternative external provider.

Ideally, the purchaser should have the right or "option" to renew at a predetermined price that was agreed to when the contract was initially entered into. Avoid the "automatic renewal" trap where the burden is on the pur-chaser to take affirmative steps (typically within a short time frame) to avoid being "locked" into a renewal. Remember that even if you have the option to renew at favorable pricing, you may want to begin "negotiations" a year or more before the agreement ends. Whatever the arrangement, keeping track of when the agreement will expire is crucial.

If "locking in" the pricing for the renewal term is not possible, the external provider should at least be required to notify the purchaser of the proposed pricing at least twelve (12) months prior to renewal.

19. TERM AND RIGHT TO RENEW CLAUSES

The following type of clause is one way the parties can address the issue of duration and renewals. Check with your counsel in particular situations.

1. *INITIAL TERM AND RIGHT TO RENEW*

The initial term of this Agreement shall be [_____ ( ) years] beginning on _____ and ending on _____ (the "Initial Term"). Company shall have the right, at its option, to renew this Agreement for one or more subsequent term(s) (the "Subsequent Terms").

2. *DURATION OF SUBSEQUENT TERM(S).*

Should the Company elect to exercise its right to renew this Agreement, the du-ration of any such Subsequent Term shall be, at the Company's option, either: 1) _____ year(s) in duration ("Option 1") or 2) equal to the period of the Initial Term ("Option 2").

3. *PRICING FOR SUBSEQUENT TERM(S).*

Not less than [one (1) year] prior to the expiration of the Initial Term, or any Subsequent Terms, Contractor shall provide Company with written pricing proposals covering the Subsequent Term under either or both Options 1 and 2, as requested by the Company. Company shall either accept or reject said pricing proposals for Options 1 or 2 or negotiate with Contractor in an effort to reach mutually acceptable pricing for any Subsequent Terms. Pricing proposals shall be no less favorable than those being offered to any other entity for the same services in comparable quantities.

4. *EXTENSION OF EXISTING AGREEMENT.*

In the event the Partie(s) not reach Agreement on pricing for any Subsequent Terms, and the Agreement expires while the parties are in negotiations, the Company shall have the right to renew this Agreement on a month-to-month basis under the existing pricing for a period not to exceed six (6) months or as long as the Parties are in negotiations, whichever is longer.

20. PRICING SERVICES OVER THE LONG TERM

Outsourcing contracts tend to be relatively long-term. It is notoriously difficult to price services over the long term. Progressive (automatic price increases every year) or escalating (price increases tied to an index) pricing each have serious drawbacks and should not be the basis of price revisions.

Increasing prices every year may not reflect the supplier's actual change (either increases or decreases) in cost. Ideally, process improvements and better technologies should drive cost (and pricing) down over time. Cost structure, total cost, and price discipline analysis needs to be brought to bear.

Escalation clauses tied to an index, such as one of the two "Consumer Price Indexes" prepared by the Bureau of Labor Statistics, may bear absolutely no relationship to the supplier's actual costs. This is because indexes tend to be broad-based and made up of components that do not affect the supplier's costs. Keeping the term of the agreement relatively short with the option to renew for subsequent terms if favorable pricing can be agreed upon is a better approach.

21. LIQUIDATED DAMAGES

When at the time a contract is entered into, the damages due to a breach would be very difficult to determine, the parties can agree that a certain dollar amount will be payable as liquidated damages for the breach. However, this amount must be a reasonable forecast of the damages caused by the breach and be compensatory rather than punitive in nature.

Since liquidated damages operate as a "cap" or limit on liability, it is important that the amount is not set so low as to be an attractive "option" not to perform. By the same token, liquidated damages cannot be set so high as to amount to an unenforceable penalty or punishment for breach. Remember that although liquidated damages eliminate the need to prove the dollar amount of the damages, the fact of the breach must still be established.

Liquidated damages are especially well suited to situations like outsourcing agreements where there are (or should be) clearly defined deliverables such as specified service levels, work volumes, milestones, due dates, or response and turnaround times. Be sure to specify whether the liquidated damages apply to all or just certain breaches. For example, you can set liquidated damages for delay but still recover actual damages for other types of breaches or damages where the dollar amount of damages are easier to prove. In an outsourcing context, you are really seeking to keep the external provider's attention focused on service. Note that you can have liquidated damages, but not incentives payments, or you can have both. There is no legal or logical requirement that you have incentive payments (which are compensation for doing well) just because the parties have stipulated damages in the event of a breach.

Where the parties elect to use liquidated damages, the contract should reflect the following type of language. Consult with counsel regarding the specific language to use.

<u>Liquidated Damages</u>

> *The parties agree that in the event of [specify the beach] the harm to the corporation would be very difficult or impracticable to accurately estimate and that the amount fixed as liquidated damages is not a penalty, but a reasonable forecast of just compensation for said harm.*

22. LEASES AND LICENSES

1. *ANTICIPATE OUTSOURCING.*

Some leases and licenses restrict use or access to the signatories and forbid any use by or "assignment" to third parties. Even if a corporation has no current plans to outsource, the possibility of outsourcing a particular function in the future needs to be considered. For example, equipment or office leases and software licenses should be negotiated to reflect that the items, space or software can be used by an external provider at no additional charge or expense.

2. *MANAGE SOFTWARE RIGHTS AND LIABILITY.*

Where the external provider will be using software to deliver the out-sourced services, software licensing issues loom large. Properly managing software rights are a critical part of any outsourcing effort. Accordingly:

1. Avoid violating existing licensing agreements, and

2. Avoid overdependence by preserving the corporation's ability to "transition back" in-house or "migrate" to another supplier.

If the software to be used by the corporation is proprietary to the corporation (i.e., all copyright or other intellectual property rights are vested in the corporation, as opposed to merely licensed to the corporation), the corporation is free to permit the external provider to use its software. In effect, the corporation should license its software to the external provider for the limited purpose of supporting the outsourcing agreement. Most of the time, however, any software to be used will be owned by someone other than the corporation. Protecting the corporation's rights in an outsourcing arrangement involving software will, therefore, require that the Corporation:

1. License any software owned by the corporation to the external provider.

2. Secure, if necessary, the right for the external provider to use software licensed to the Corporation.

3. Retain the right to approve what software the external provider will use and escrow the software source code.

4. Retain the right to use software supplied by the external provider in the event the agreement is terminated (for any reason under any circumstances).

3. OUTSOURCING AND LICENSES

Where an external provider may need to use software licensed to the corporation from a third party, i.e., software licensor, the following type of language can be included in the license: Check with counsel as to the proper wording to use in individual cases.

Use of Licensed Software

Licensee shall have the right to grant access to and use of the licensed software to outsourcing contractors or other third parties for the purpose of performing data processing or related services for Licensee provided said persons or entities agree to respect the proprietary nature of said software. Licensee shall have the right to install and use the licensed software on computers and related equipment used, owned, or leased by the outsourcing contractor.

23. AVOID THE ASSIGNMENT "TRAP"

1. ANTICIPATE CHANGES IN CORPORATE STRUCTURE

Corporations are changing and evolving in an effort to become more competitive. Accordingly, management needs to anticipate the possibility that a particular function may one day be sold or "spun-off" to an affiliate, subsidiary, or other legal entity. Thus, leases and licenses being negotiated today need to reflect that contingency.

2. RETAIN THE RIGHT TO REJECT ASSIGNMENT TO A THIRD PARTY

Note that although it might make sense for the recipient of services to have the right to transfer or assign its rights under the agreement to another entity, the same is not true for the external provider. Having made a careful selection and picked the supplier based on its special expertise, corporations should not be required to accept services from another entity. By analogy, if you hired "Michelangelo" to paint your portrait, you do want him to assign that obligation to "Harry the Painter". By contrast, as long as Michelangelo gets paid, he shouldn't care whose portrait he paints, yours or someone else's.

24. KEY PERSONNEL

1. THE PROVIDER'S EMPLOYEES

Making a careful selection includes ensuring that claims match its actual capabilities. Although an organization may look good on paper and have an excellent reputation, individuals can and often do make the difference. Key personnel to be supplied by the external provider should be carefully screened and selected. Once assigned to the project, these personnel develop insights that may be hard to duplicate or take time to transfer to another person. Placing reasonable restrictions on a supplier's ability to assign and reassign key personnel to other projects can protect continuity and the working relationship that has developed. There should be an understanding and disincentive against having key staff personnel pulled off to go work on "hot" projects elsewhere.

2. THE PURCHASER'S EMPLOYEES

"Key personnel" also includes certain Company employees. For example, the Company employees who were intimately involved in the selection of the outsourcing provider and the negotiation of the contract will need to continue to play a key role in the administration and interpretation of the contract. It is inevitable, that over time, uncertainty (or even serious disagreements) will develop about what the parties intended in terms of scope of work, respective responsibilities, performance levels, and the like. It is often difficult to perfectly reflect all nuances in a written document. Thus, the Company's negotiators and other key personnel should continue to be involved on the Company's behalf in interpreting administration and the outsourcing contract.

25. CAPTURING ALL VERBAL REPRESENTATIONS

Like all contracts, outsourcing agreements contain "entire agreement" or "integration" clauses designed to exclude any written or verbal representations (what lawyers call "parol evidence") that purport to vary or contradict the terms of the written agreement. Such clauses typically recite words to the effect that "This agreement is our entire and only agreement, and no other document or statements are part of the agreement."

Despite such clauses, many purchasers rely on the external supplier's verbal representations in making their decisions. To compound the problem, the parties seldom have identical recollections as to who said what to whom and when. Moreover, even assuming total recall, verbal representations are often subject to different interpretations.

Avoid problems by making sure all important representations, whether written or spoken - end up being included or incorporated into the final written agreement. If the proposal is going to be incorporated into the contract, remember to have the external provider amend or update its proposal to reflect any improvements made during the course of negotiations and verify that this has, in fact, been done. As they say: "Trust, but verify".

26. DATA OWNERSHIP AND RETURN

The outsourcing agreement should specify that the external supplier shall return the corporation's proprietary or confidential data and information upon either expiration or termination, whether for cause or convenience. The Agreement should also specify the form and the means by which the data should be returned. After the data has been returned, the external provider should be required to delete any remaining data belonging to the corporation from the external provider's files.

The return of such data or information should not be contingent upon whether the corporation has complied with its obligations under the agreement, since this can be a subjective determination. One way to protect the corporation against being disadvantaged by not having access to its own data is to require the external provider to periodically provide copies to the corporation or to an escrow agent.

27. BUYBACK AND BUYOUT OPTIONS

The "transition back" plan should anticipate the possibility that the corporation may one day wish to recapture or "buyback" any assets sold to the external provider, as well as a "buyout" of the external provider's investment in the effort. The price or valuation method for exercising such "buyback" or "buyout" options should be negotiated up front as part of the outsourcing agreement.

28. LABOR CONTRACT RESTRICTIONS

Bear in mind that certain labor contracts may have varying restrictions on outsourcing work. Checking with the proper persons as to the existence and extent of any such restrictions should be part of the due diligence, planning, and approval process when exploring outsourcing opportunities.

29. OUTSOURCING MEANS CONTINUOUS CONTRACT MANAGEMENT

Whatever the duration of the Agreement, the communication process should not end with the signing of the Agreement. Managing the outsourcing relationship involves continuous and ongoing negotiation due to differences as to what is within scope and changes in needs or requirements. Once the deal is signed and a corporation's facilities, systems, or personnel are turned over to an external provider, these negotiations will shift from a competitive environment to what is, in effect, a single-source procurement. Hence the need to structure long-term outsourcing agreements on measurable performance based pricing so that disputes are minimized and changes managed. Corporations can maintain at least some leverage throughout the relationship by keeping the term relatively short, outsourcing selectively, and having a well-planned exit strategy (transition back plan).

30. OUTSOURCING GUIDELINES

The following guidelines may be helpful in structuring outsourcing transactions:

1. *SPECIFY PERFORMANCE LEVELS AND TARGETS.*

   If appropriate, use current performance as a baseline from which to measure improvement.

2. *SPECIFY HOW PERFORMANCE WILL BE MEASURED.*

   Define the measurement criteria, as well as the form and frequency of reporting requirements. Consider using "customer satisfaction" based on survey results as one means of measuring performance.

3. *INTEGRATE THE COMPANY'S BUSINESS PLAN AND OBJECTIVES.*

Make sure the agreement reflects your business plan and objectives and is flexible enough to accommodate change.

4. *TIE PAYMENT TO PERFORMANCE.*

Structure payment provisions to reward performance, share savings, and provide incentives, but set liquidated damages for non-performance.

5. *ANTICIPATE INCREASES AND DECREASES IN SCOPE OR COSTS.*

Particularly in long-term contracts, structure pricing to reflect changes in scope and cost.

6. *ALLOW THE OUTSOURCER TO MAKE A REASONABLE PROFIT.*

Expect the outsourcer to make a profit, but require candid discussion and disclosure of costs, as well as "open-book" accounting.

7. *ACTIVELY MANAGE THE CONTRACT AND RELATIONSHIP.*

Don't abdicate responsibility. Have a continuous and active focus on performance levels, solving problems and making improvements, as well as shared objectives.

8. *TAKE THE TIME TO DO IT RIGHT.*

Balance the desire to quickly make improvements against the need to clearly define the respective responsibilities of the parties.

9. *THINK OF THE END AT THE BEGINNING.*

Anticipate and plan for the day that the relationship will end and that the services will be performed by someone else or "migrate" back to the Company.

31. MANAGING THE CONTRACT

As with any commercial transaction, a contract which clearly defines the respective rights and responsibilities of the parties is critical to the success of the effort. It follows that if the parties have expended the time and effort to negotiate a detailed agreement with specific service levels and deliverables, the parties (and especially the purchaser) have a strong financial and operational interest in ensuring that the terms of the deal are followed. Since the contract contains the criteria by which performance is measured, it is imperative that the outsourcing agreement be followed and used as part of the ongoing operations and not simply filed and forgotten. As they say, "You can't manage what you aren't measuring". Nor can you measure (or manage) what you haven't read.

Often the person who had been involved in managing the outsourced department or function is assigned to manage the outsourcing contract. However, managing a department or function, with its heavy emphasis on managing employees or company facilities, does not necessarily include the skill sets required to manage the contract and the relationship with the external provider.

32. DELEGATION VS. ACCOUNTABILITY

One important caveat cannot be over stressed. Outsourcing does not lessen a manager's ultimate accountability. Although one can delegate execution or performance to an external provider, the responsible manager is always accountable, regardless of whether the function is performed "in-house" or on an outsourced basis.

33. CONCLUSION

Outsourcing has both potential advantages and pitfalls which need to be carefully considered and managed. A clear and complete articulation of the parties' respective responsibilities in the form of a well-conceived agreement, as well as a proper contract administration and management, are key to ensuring a successful outsourcing effort.

Note an emerging trend back to in-sourcing. As companies come to value both the tangible and intangible benefits of greater control and employee loyalty, many organizations are reducing or backing away from outsourcing.

STRATEGIC ALLIANCES

Intense and global competition, as well as relentless technological and regulatory change is forcing corporations to find ways to get stronger quickly. In order to meet these challenges, corporations are asking themselves four basic questions:

1. What do we seek to obtain via "strategic alliance"?

2. What are the potential "merger and acquisition" opportunities?

3. What do we keep or develop "in-house" from internal resources?

4. What and how do we purchase from "suppliers" on a "commodity" basis?

These questions reflect that there are essentially four basic sources on which to draw in attempting to move from "best efforts" to the "best": internal resources; procurement transactions; mergers and acquisitions; and; strategic alliances.

INTERNAL RESOURCES

Few, if any, corporations have the luxury of having all the resources needed to compete in a changing global economy from purely internal sources. Of necessity, even the largest and strongest international corporations will be looking for external resources to help them achieve their goals and objectives.

PROCUREMENT TRANSACTIONS

Lots of money can be saved by leveraging buying power in order to take advantage of economies of scale, controlling inventory costs, and practicing total costs management. But contract management alone will not necessarily build competitive strength.

MERGERS AND ACQUISITIONS

Mergers and acquisitions are usually highly complex and costly undertakings. In a merger or acquisition, the entire function is purchased including what is good, bad, needed, or unneeded. Highly attractive candidates also command a premium.

STRATEGIC ALLIANCES

Strategic alliances are based on the notion that they can be a quick way to lower costs, spread risk and gain access to resources or markets. Often, cooperation can be a way to "cheaper, faster, better" means of doing things. Both parties can take advantage of the other party's strengths and build competitive strength together based on sharing control and costs.

STRUCTURING STRATEGIC ALLIANCES

Strategic alliance can take on the form of a separate legal entity, such as a corporation, partnership, or joint venture, or can be based on a contractual relationship. Although important, the form of organization is not as important as having clearly defined respective responsibilities, knowing how decisions will be made, and having a mechanism for solving problems or disputes. The key is to have a mutual business plan with specific goals and defined boundaries.

Successful strategic alliances are built on communication. The parties need to be able to build trust and understand how they will work together. Key personnel and teams will thus play a critical role. However, communication needs to be clear, coordinated, and focused. Inconsistency and conflicting signals can create serious confusion. The idea is to limit the number and points of interface to ensure that the correct information is communicated to the proper persons in a timely manner.

ADVANTAGES OF STRATEGIC ALLIANCES

Cooperation can be quicker and far less expensive and risky than independently developing new technology, products or markets. Yet, both parties can continue to pursue their own strategies by having both mutual and separate objectives. Essentially, strategic allies use key parts or aspects of their respective organization's present strengths to build new or future strengths and synergies.

Cooperation can also allow the parties to more effectively compete with their competitors by sharing costs, resources, and information. While cooperation has its risks, those risks (e.g., loss of control and skills, overdependence, etc. . .) need to be balanced against the risk of going it alone.

Typically, the longer something takes, the more it costs. Moreover, the consequences of being "late" to market can have an adverse impact on success and profitability. Strategic alliances can speed development and marketing, thereby cutting the time it takes to bring new products or services to market, reducing the period from "concept to customer".

HOW STRATEGIC ALLIANCES WORK

The world economy has become a single integrated market with sets of corporations competing against other sets of corporations. In order to meet competition, corporation are seeking to:

1. Spread risk

2. Lower costs

3. Increase revenues, and

4. Release internal resources

by forming strategic alliances with competitors with:

1. Compatible cultures

2. Complimentary resources

3. Mutual needs and interests

4. Shared goals and objectives

so as to gain competitive advantages through cooperation. These competitive advantages can include:

1. Reducing the time from "concept to customer"

2. Creating new, improved, or cheaper products

3. Gaining better and quicker access to markets

4. More efficient use and allocation of resources

HOW TO PROTECT ONE'S INTERESTS IN A STRATEGIC ALLIANCE: INDEPENDENCE THROUGH MUTUAL DEPENDENCE

Every corporation has its own set of core competencies which are the source of its competitive advantage and the ability to create value. Strategic alliances should be structured so that each firm will retain or increase its separate and unique ability to add value. As long as both parties need each other, the alliance is sure to survive and has the best chance of being successful. An alliance which weakens or gives away control of a core competency is not worth the risk.

The road to dependency can start in several ways: Over time, one party may acquire the other party's core competencies or take over all the complex tasks that add value. Unless core strengths are protected and unless both parties participate in value-adding activities, one party will eventually dominate or even acquire the other. Shifting responsibilities to the other party will eventually reduce the ability to perform that responsibility.

The best way to preserve mutual dependence is to hang on to the sources of core strengths that provide a competitive advantage. Each firm's core strengths will be somewhat unique, but will typically fall into one or more of the following categories.

1. Expertise in the business/industry
2. Property - which is valuable or strategic
3. Access - to markets, customers, facilities
4. Products - which are unique or proprietary
5. Finances - sources of funding or cash flow
6. Information - such as customer information
7. Operations - such as systems or infrastructure
8. Goodwill - positive market image or brand name
9. Implementation - efficient decision making process
10. Intellectual rights - patents, copyrights, trade secrets

If both parties depend on each other to add value by contributing this unique "core competencies", they are more likely to have a successful strategic alliance.

ALLIANCE OR ACQUISITION?

1. When does it make sense to enter into a strategic alliance as opposed to a merger and acquisition ("M & A")?

An outright acquisition makes the most sense when there is a lot of duplication or overlap between the parties' skills, products, customers, or markets. By contrast, a strategic alliance other than an outright acquisition, is most appropriate when the parties' respective resources or operations complement one another and create "synergies" and a better "strategic fit".

2. When is a strategic alliance likely to lead to an eventual sale?

Most of the time. The average life span of a strategic alliance is seven years (7 years) and eighty percent (80%) ultimately end in a sale by one of the parties. Thus, a "strategic alliance" may actually be a forced sale leading to an eventual transfer of ownership. Parties who are unaware of this risk and fail to anticipate the "end game" may well end up unwittingly "betting the ranch."

3. What are the typical "paths" to an unplanned sale or dissolution?

The following types of alliances have a high probability of being short-lived and not achieving their objectives: 1) alliances between two strong companies competing in their core business; 2) alliances between two weak companies; 3) alliances between a strong and a weak company, and 4) alliances where bargaining power shifts to one side. The message: Alliances between two strong and complementary partners are the most likely to lead to a long-term and mutually beneficial relationship.

SOME HARD TRUTHS ABOUT STRATEGIC ALLIANCES

1. Roughly half (50%) are successful.
2. Every partner represents a potential competitor.
3. Alliances between strong and weak parties rarely work.
4. The ability to avoid or resolve conflicts are key to success.
5. Money counts, but not as much as customers or know-how.
6. Most parties underestimate the amount of planning needed.
7. Alliances with weak or marginal players should be avoided.
8. Most alliances experience major problems in the first two years.
9. Alliances with equal ownership (50-50) are more likely to work.
10. Most alliances, even successful ones, terminate within seven years.

11. Safeguarding intellectual property/proprietary rights can be difficult.

12. About eighty percent (80%) of alliances end in acquisition by a party.

SOME DO'S AND DON'TS OF STRATEGIC ALLIANCES

1. Don't partner with the goal of improving your skills.
2. Don't partner with direct competitors in your core business.
3. Don't partner with the objective of raising capital without giving up control.
4. Don't partner with a weak partner with the expectation of fixing problems together.
5. Don't partner with the objective of minimizing investments in core competencies.
6. Do identify and evaluate the parties' respective strengths and contributions.
7. Do be mindful that the partner who wants to sell is at a distinct disadvantage.
8. Do anticipate the possibility and guard against a shift in bargaining strength.
9. Do build on distinctive strengths, as opposed to trying to fill gaps in core business or markets.
10. Do anticipate conflict and the possibility of a stalemate on important issues leading to acquisition or dissolution.

CONCLUSION: WARNING; HIGH FAILURE RATE

As in the case of mergers and acquisitions, about half of all strategic alliances fail to achieve their initial objectives and end up adversely affecting productivity and profitability.

Typically, short-term "one shot" savings, do not translate into long-term gains. Poor "partner" selection decisions, unrealized gains due to mismanagement, unforeseen changes or circumstances, underestimating difficulties, overemphasis on "doing the deal" and insufficient planning are frequent causes of failure. Moreover, owing to the many unpredictable variations and circumstances, experienced firms experience roughly the same rate of success/failure as do inexperienced firms. Accordingly, great care needs to be taken when contemplating strategic alliances.

APPLYING A LESSON'S LEARNED METHODOLOGY

Every good procurement professional understands that a big part of success is improving by: (a) repeating successful behaviors and approaches and (b) learning from mistakes made in the past. This can only be achieved by having a disciplined lesson's learned methodology as part of the procurement process.

LESSON'S LEARNED DEFINED

A lesson learned is useful project or transaction related information gained through experience. It can be a valuable technique or approach that you used to achieve a desired outcome that you can repeat or tailor to your procurement process or it can be an undesirable result you wish to avoid in the future.

Ask questions to identify lessons learned... "What worked well or what didn't work so well?"

LESSONS LEARNED CATEGORIES

Acquired by an innovation or process improvement

Learned from adverse experience that is reduced to a process

Learned from a positive experience that is reduced to a process

HOW DO YOU USE LESSONS LEARNED?

Lessons learned are used to improve the procurement process.

A team approach to documenting and communicating lessons learned can help a Company incorporate lessons learned into a process.

Your team needs to be a "learning organization" and cannot overlook its own experiences as a basis for improvement.

Do not assume that your collective experiences are passed along to the next person or group. Mistakes or missed opportunities tend to be repeated.

To be considered a learning organization companies must be proactive, capture lessons learned, and "cross-pollinate" the concepts. This is best achieved through documentation and training that exposes the information to others who may benefit from it. A structured way to pass on this information is needed to create a "learning organization".

Incorporating lessons learned into a process helps organizations operate with less risk, increased efficiency and more adaptability.

HOW TO DOCUMENT LESSONS LEARNED

Documenting useful lessons learned requires a clear understanding of the successes and/or failures of a project or transaction.

Because lessons learned serve as an important management tool in gaining organizational knowledge, managing risk, and improving performance, they must be relevant to future projects or transactions.

To build relevance into your lessons-learned consider:

Identifying the circumstances in which the problem arose; and,

Describing how the problem arose and define the problem or positive development encountered, and provide concrete, practical solutions or recommendations based on this experience.

Statements such as "Clearly defined roles and responsibilities, along with a strong focus on communication channels, are essential to success" are not effective lessons learned. There is no context for such statements, and without context such statements are of little use.

While requiring more effort to develop, the examples in the template make the same statement, but do so in a context that defines what management element is affected by the lesson learned, what the problem was that led to the lesson being learned, and how the lesson learned can serve future endeavors or projects before a problem arises.

WHAT IS REQUIRED FOR A LESSON LEARNED?

In order to be easily accessible and beneficial across your organization, lessons learned should have the same look and content. Just as it is important that procurement professionals have a common understanding of the practices and terminology employed in their profession, it is equally important that the lessons learned they contribute be presented in a manner that is easily understood by their peers, successors and decision makers.

LESSONS LEARNED TEMPLATE

The template below contains a sample template and directions for recording lessons learned for your organization and for the use of others:

LESSONS LEARNED TEMPLATE	
Operating Unit:	
Project Name:	
Point of Contact (POC): Name, phone, email.	
Which management areas are involved? (Integration, scope, time, cost, execution, project controls, quality, human resources, communications, risk, procurement.)	
Briefly describe the problem or situation including any relevant context such as stage of project.	
How was the problem resolved or the process improved?	
Lesson learned: How can this problem can be avoided in the future or how can the process be improved?	

SAMPLE FORM OF CONTRACT STRUCTURE

*CONTRACT FOR [*DESCRIBE*]*
Dated as of [*month, day, year*]
between
[*Name of Company*]
and
[*Name of Contractor*]

SAMPLE FORM OF CONTRACT STRUCTURE

There is no perfect way to structure a contract but the following illustrates a perfectly sound and logical way of doing so. The importance is for each organization to have their preferred method in place provided it meets the organizations needs and is consistently applied and followed. Inconsistent contracting structure leads to confusion and difficulty in sound contract management.

This [*identify Contract*] (the "Contract"), dated as of [*Month, day, and year*], is by and between [*identify the name of Company, corporate form (LLC, Inc., JV, LLP, etc.) and mailing address*], (the "Company"), and [*identify the name of Contractor, corporate form (LLC, Inc., JV, LLP, etc.) and mailing address*] (the "Contractor"), collectively referred to as the "Parties". Company and Contractor are the only Parties to the Contract.

RECITALS:

WHEREAS, [*Provide brief introduction/background to Contract*]

WHEREAS, [*Continue brief introduction/background to Contract*]

WHEREAS, [*Continue brief introduction/background to Contract*]

NOW, THEREFORE, in consideration of the mutual promises contained herein, and for other good and valuable consideration, the sufficiency of which is hereby acknowledged, the Parties, intending to be legally bound, agree as follows:

1. Contract Documents. This Contract includes the Exhibits listed below, including their Attachments, which as a whole, constitute the entire agreement between the Parties, all of which form one integrated agreement:

    a. Exhibit A – Contractor's Scope of Work

    b. Exhibit B – Contractor's Compensation Schedule

    c. Exhibit C – Contract Commercial Terms and Conditions

    d. Exhibit D – [*other Exhibits such as Parental Guarantee, Insurance Certificates, Performance and Payment Bonds, Performance Schedules, Testing and Acceptance protocols, or other requirements not covered in previous Exhibits.*]

2. Order of Precedence. The sections or parts of this Contract are to be considered complementary and what is required by one will be binding as if required by all. In the event of a conflict between the Exhibits, the order of precedence shall be: [*specify*]. In the event of a conflict within an Exhibit, the most stringent requirement will take precedence, except as may be otherwise determined in writing by the Company.

3. Headings. Any table of contents or section, article, attachment and exhibit titles and headings are inserted for convenience only and shall not be used for the purposes of interpreting this Contract.

4. <u>Plural and Singular</u>. Words importing the singular also include the plural and vice versa.

5. <u>Without Limitation</u>. The words "include" and "including" are not words of limitation and shall be deemed to be followed by the words "but not limited to."

6. <u>Reference to Contract</u>. The words "herein", "hereof," or "hereunder" or similar terms refer to this Contract as a whole and not to any specific section or article.

7. <u>Contract Price</u>. As full consideration to the Contractor for the full and complete performance of the Work and all costs incurred in connection therewith, Company shall pay, and the Contractor shall accept the compensation set forth in Exhibit B.

8. <u>Optional Work and Pricing</u>. [*Address if and as appropriate.*]

9. <u>Entire Agreement</u>. This Contract constitutes the full, complete and only agreement between the Parties and their affiliates with respect to the Work. This Contract supersedes any course of performance, course of dealings, usage of trade, previous agreements, representations, understandings, either oral or written between the Parties and their affiliates. No terms, conditions, agreements, representations, understandings, course of performance, course of dealing, or usage of trade purporting to modify, vary, supplement, explain, or amend any provisions of this Contract shall be effective unless in writing, in the form of a Company Change Order executed in accordance with the provisions herein. If any part of this Contract is determined to be judicially unenforceable for any reason, the remainder of this Contract shall remain in full force and effect.

10. <u>Authority to Sign</u>. The signatories hereto represent that they are authorized to enter into this Contract on behalf of the Party for whom they sign.

IN WITNESS WHEREOF, the Parties have caused this Contract to be executed as of the date first above written.

[CONTRACTOR]   *[COMPANY]*

By: _____   <u>By</u>: _____
        (Signature)   (Signature)

Name: _____   Name: _____

Title: _____   Title: _____

<u>Date</u>: _____   Date: _____

INDEX

Made in the USA
Columbia, SC
27 July 2017